ASCD
IN
RETROSPECT

Contributions to the History of the
Association for Supervision and Curriculum Development

Edited by William Van Til

ASCD

Association for Supervision and Curriculum Development
125 N. West Street
Alexandria, Virginia

ASCD publications present a variety of viewpoints. The views expressed or implied
in this publication are not necessarily official positions of the Association.

ASCD Editors:
Nancy Carter Modrak
Jo Ann Irick Jones

Price: $8.00
ASCD Stock Number: 611-86014
ISBN: 0-87120-135-6
Library of Congress
  Card Catalog No.: 86-70116

ASCD in Retrospect

Foreword

Those engaged in the interrelated crafts of supervision, curriculum, and instruction are often criticized by scholars and practitioners alike for being unfamiliar with their traditions. We urge those critics and our participants in those crafts to know those traditions through the following pages, which illuminate the path of development of the Association for Supervision and Curriculum Development. ASCD has served well to focus the talents, energies, and values of the individuals it represents. Moreover, it has provided the forum, structure, and opportunities for them to bring to fruition many of the pioneering concepts that make ASCD unique. In truth, the history of ASCD is the history of supervision, curriculum, and instruction. Over the years, the Association has served as the heart, mind, conscience, and perhaps soul of these fields.

The decision by the Executive Council to bring together into a single volume the record of the development of our Association was significant. The invitation to the incomparable William Van Til to serve as editor and to gather other former presidents and leaders as contributors has resulted in a product far more powerful than anyone anticipated.

The authors share their recollection of events in which they themselves played important parts. I have found their chronicle fascinating and comprehensive. I know that all ASCD members and others wishing to understand the vitality and essence of the organization will find these pages exciting and illuminating.

The volume captures both the spirit and substance that comprise ASCD. Bill Van Til speaks of the caring and vision that are the essence of our efforts as an organization. Galen Saylor traces our roots and exalts the merger of practitioners and professors that provides the life blood of ASCD.

The views of supervision and curriculum development during both early and later years, including our involvement in group process; our championing of social forces, ethnic groups, and the humanist movements; and our continuing commitment to look into the years ahead provide heartening and accurate perspective.

For every milestone, the chronicle is told with the respect for accuracy and attention to detail that could be provided only by those who experienced those significant events. Their reports offer convincing evidence that ASCD has often reflected internally the disparate forces and factors with which the total enterprise of education itself has been confronted. The volume is sometimes appropriately critical, frequently unsettled, never dull.

The excitement and the unflinching honesty of *ASCD in Retrospect* emerge in the writers' personal recollections of growing up professionally within the organization; of being nurtured by crusading leaders, challenging programs, and broad-based member participation; and of experiencing the hard-earned increases in number of members, scope of activity, and degree of influence.

In spanning 40 years, the accounts of this volume provide a microcosm of American education and the broader culture. Throughout their reports, the writers remain in touch with society past and present and occasionally anticipate potential issues and emerging trends.

For the former members of ASCD who have given themselves in service to us, the volume is a fitting memorial; for the present members who have lived many of those events, it is an appropriate record; and for recent members and those still to join us, it is an outstanding orientation.

When the next such volume is written, we can only hope that it will equal in quality the work of these chroniclers. You are cordially invited to be a part of the venture and adventure they describe.

GERALD R. FIRTH
ASCD President, 1986-87

ASCD: An Introduction

WILLIAM VAN TIL
President, 1961-62

The quest for an organization that would be socially oriented, responsive to the needs of learners, and committed to democratic values attracted some educators of the 1940s to the Association for Supervision and Curriculum Development. We sought an association open to all who would work for good school programs through curriculum improvement and helpful supervision. We wanted to belong to an organization that would foster both informed discussion and effective action for better schools and a better society. To us, the National Education Association seemed too much dominated by conservative school superintendents; the program of the separate subject matter organizations too specialized; the membership of the NEA department enrolling supervisors and directors of instruction too limited. So when the independent Society for Curriculum Study and the NEA's Department of Supervisors and Directors of Instruction merged in 1943 into a newly created department—part of the NEA family of organizations yet independent as to programs and policies—we welcomed the opportunity to participate.

The new group created by the 1943 merger was first titled the Department of Supervision and Curriculum Development. As a social studies teacher in the Ohio State University School, I hoped that the new organization would deal with social realities and respond to social forces, as well as foster humane values and recognize the interests of children and youth. Consequently, I welcomed a request from Gordon Mackenzie and Cecil Parker for a chapter for the new Department's first yearbook, the 1944 *Toward a New Curriculum*.

Any uncertainty as to the social orientation of the new organization vanished when, two years later, I contributed to a yearbook published under the new name, Association for Supervision and Curriculum Development. I found Lelia Ann Taggart and Fred T. Wilhelms, co-editors of the 1946 *Leadership Through Supervision*, supportive of the analysis of the culture that constituted much of my chapter. (Only in 1985, while editing this book, did I realize that I had contributed the first chapter to the first yearbook ever published by ASCD!)

So I became an active participant in the Association and began to shift from specialization in social studies to the broader field of curriculum development. In the more than 40 years that followed my first experiences in the organization, ASCD has continued to demonstrate social concern and commitment to better education in its activities. Again and again the organization has recognized the interdependence of curricular sources derived from social, psychological, and philosophical foundations. ASCD has a long history of support for a balanced curriculum and effective leadership practices.

Seldom have ASCD's convictions been as well expressed as at the close of ASCD's first decade. While the Progressive Education Association was disbanding in 1955 (in part because of dissension over whether education should be child-centered or socially centered, should employ indoctrination or use the method of intelligence), ASCD was presenting to the 1955 business meeting a carefully thought-through platform of beliefs. Officially adopted in 1956, the platform read in part:

ASCD believes that
—the public schools are our chief and most effective means of developing free men capable of solving problems and governing themselves successfully;
—in a democracy, society has an obligation to provide free and equal education opportunities for all children and youth, and the learner, according to his ability, has an obligation to take advantage of the educational opportunities offered;
—the main purpose of the American schools is to provide for the fullest possible development of each learner for living morally, creatively, and productively in a democratic society;
—the curriculum, consisting of all the experiences of the learner under the guidance of the school, is effective in achieving the purpose of education when it is based on the needs of the learner and the demands of the society in which he lives;
—because of individual differences, social change, and the nature of the educative process, continuous planning, development, and appraisal of the curriculum are essential;
—growth in realization of democratic values requires that learners have freedom to learn and the teachers have freedom to teach.

The platform then called for cooperative planning and action by all, including teachers and learners; leadership and coordination by supervisors, curriculum directors, and principals; cooperative interaction between school and community; mutual respect, democratic human relations, and growth by all involved in curriculum improvement.

ASCD learned early to exert influence on schools and society through committees, conferences, the resolutions process, publications, governing bodies, and staff. In 1945-46, while the new organization was still titled a department, 20 committees with members from 12 regions were established. At the first annual national conference in 1946, ASCD found that meetings of these work groups were effective ways of involving members; thereafter, throughout ASCD's history, working groups, committees, and commissions have often taken positions, recommended publications, issued statements, and influenced ASCD's governing bodies and their policies. The voice of the membership was heard through the resolutions process, which was first instituted at the 1947 conference and annually specified courses of action for the staff when endorsed by the governing bodies. Yearbooks, pamphlets, and *Educational Leadership* voiced the views of ASCD members who contributed to the organization's publications program; recently tapes and cassettes have supplemented the written word. Governing bodies and executive secretaries have conveyed the Association's positions through media releases, communications to organizations and governmental bodies, testimony at Congressional hearings, etc.

It's hard to convey today how important ASCD was to those of us who came early to the Association. ASCD was the focus for our efforts to create better education in a better society. For us ASCD was an arena for sharing agreements and disagreements, a center for communicating to educators and the public, a place for people willing to speak out on controversial issues and to stand up to be counted, a rallying point when our views were attacked by reactionary forces, a forum for participation by all, young or old, obscure or prominent.

Fred T. Wilhelms, a former executive secretary of ASCD, said it well in 1960 in one of the memorable Importance of People columns in *Educational Leadership*. Writing on "The Importance of ASCD," he commented:

Two characteristics: caring tremendously about children and teachers and what happens when they get together; the ability to involve almost everybody; these, to me, make ASCD stand out above all other organizations. Of course, these two root down to something deeper—I don't exactly know what—a vision of what society could be, perhaps, so goading a vision that it never lets compromise be comfortable; a faith in the human person, so deep-rooted it cannot be shaken. Sometimes I feel that the "something deeper" lies very close to Albert Schweitzer's reverence for life. . . .

It is hard to realize how different American education would be today if ASCD had not been there. When the battles were going at their worst, there stood our organization. General Jackson at Bull Run, standing there "like a stone wall," was not a firmer rallying point. It makes a difference when there is a place to stand. . . .

We've been people who intuitively move toward life rather than away from it. We have a tremendous commitment to democracy, and an even deeper feeling for the lone individual inside that democracy. We're deep-dyed professionals with a terrific urge to build a school system on what we know about children and societies and learning and teaching—not by guidelines of what's safe or politic or fashionable. We're an odd crew—tough, tender, earthy, visionary, fond of each other, argumentative—and with it all everlastingly devoted to the job as it is given us to see the job.

Shakespeare's phrase, "We few, we happy few," appropriately applies to the ASCD I knew over many years. Today ASCD is no longer "we few"; in the mid-1980s the membership passed the 70,000 mark. Can ASCD maintain and extend today what may still be useful from our heritage developed in a time when the happy warriors were fewer? Now that we have grown more numerous, can we build on the past and beyond the past through envisioning and creating new approaches to better education in a better society through improved supervision and curriculum development?

This booklet has been assembled to help with such questions. It is not the definitive official history of ASCD; such a venture, beyond present funding, humanpower, and archival resources, must wait for some later day. Instead the reader will find here some contributions to ASCD's history as seen through the individual spectacles of some former ASCD presidents plus the current president and executive director. Each has written as he or she saw fit on some aspect of ASCD close to the writer's heart. No editor has requested or expected unanimity from the contributions; ASCD presidents have not always agreed on what ASCD should most emphasize in programs and as to policies, nor do they here.

Yet here is food for thought and for the spirit grown from experiences in cultivating ASCD's gardens. We hope this contribution to history will help you as you build toward your goals through ASCD.

1

ASCD and Its Beginnings

J. Galen Saylor
President, 1965-66

The Association for Supervision and Curriculum Development was created by the merger of two national professional organizations concerned about teaching, the improvement of supervision and instruction, curriculum planning, and formulating a philosophy about schooling. The Association was officially founded in March 1943; the Executive Committees of the two organizations had formally approved the merger at a meeting in Chicago on 10-11 October 1942.

The larger and older of the two organizations was the Department of Supervisors and Directors of Instruction; the other group was the Society for Curriculum Study. In 1921 a group of supervisors of instruction in some of the nation's school systems formed an organization known as The National Conference on Educational Method. In February 1928 the name was changed to National Conference of Supervisors and Directors of Instruction. In July 1929 that organization officially became a department of the National Education Association. Henceforth, it was designated as The Department of Supervisors and Directors of Instruction of the National Education Association.

The Department of Supervisors and Directors of Instruction

The object of the organization, according to its constitution, adopted in 1921, was "the improvement of supervision and teach-

Author's note: I wish to acknowledge with appreciation Hollis L. Caswell's review of this chapter.

ing." Its membership in the early years was composed principally of supervisors in city and state school systems, faculty members of colleges of education who were primarily concerned with the supervision of instruction and teaching methods in subject fields, and a few superintendents of schools who were greatly interested in the improvement of teaching. Later, especially in the 1930s, curriculum directors and personnel charged with instructional planning and college personnel teaching courses in curriculum planning and often serving as consultants to school systems organizing formal programs of curriculum development became more prevalent in the larger school systems and state departments. These educators, too, often joined the Department, and a number held leading positions in the organization by the latter 1930s.

The Department began holding annual conferences in 1921, and in the same year started publishing a journal, *Educational Method*. The journal and, in fact, the promotional literature and its conventions all emphasized "the actual work of teaching." Early issues stressed extensively the project method of teaching. The first volume contained a series of articles by the renowned William H. Kilpatrick on "the meaning of method," and on the concepts and philosophy that underlay the whole process of project teaching. Kilpatrick also served as president of the national organization in 1923-24. James F. Hosic, also of Teachers College, Columbia University, served as editor of the *Journal* from its first issue until 1939. He also served as secretary-treasurer of the organization until an office was established at the NEA in 1936, with a full-time executive-secretary.

In 1928, the Conference began the issuance of yearbooks, under the title of *Educational Supervision*. A number of the yearbooks were regarded by the profession as the best professional books on the subject of teaching and supervision.

The Society for Curriculum Study emerged from the efforts of two small, neophyte groups deeply involved in the whole matter of curriculum planning. The latter half of the 1920s was a period of intense activity, comparatively speaking, in the whole area of curriculum planning and development. Many school systems—notably Denver, Detroit, Berkeley, St. Louis, Seattle, New Orleans, Oakland, and Columbus—and a number of state departments of education— such as South Dakota, Arkansas, Alabama, and Florida—were carrying on widespread and extensive programs of curriculum construction.

The Department of Superintendence, NEA, issued two lengthy yearbooks on the curriculum of the elementary school and curriculum development programs in the nation's school systems (1924-1926). The monumental Twenty-Sixth Yearbook of the National Society for the Study of Education in two volumes, *The Foundation and Techniques of Curriculum Construction*, prepared under the editorship of Harold Rugg, was issued in 1927. The nationally acclaimed leaders in the field of curriculum planning of this period were extensively engaged in research and publication of the first major books devoted to the subject of curriculum planning. They included Franklin Bobbitt, W. W. Charters, Harold Rugg, William H. Kilpatrick, Charles Judd, Hollis L. Caswell, Doak Campbell, and L. Thomas Hopkins. Leading colleges of education were developing and offering courses in curriculum planning. It was an interesting and exciting period for forward-looking educators.

The Society for Curriculum Study

It was in this setting that two groups of educators actively engaged in curriculum planning and development and in research in the field established formal professional organizations. One group's membership primarily encompassed college personnel and the other one public school curriculum workers.

Henry Harap of Western Reserve University initiated the formation of the college organization in 1928, when he proposed to W. W. Charters that a select group of people be invited to join such a group. The response was favorable, and the leaders met in Cleveland in February 1929 to establish the National Society of Curriculum Workers. W. W. Charters was elected chair and Henry Harap secretary. During 1929, 49 persons were elected to membership.

Meanwhile, exact dates unknown, a number of directors of curriculum in public school systems and state departments of education had formed a loosely organized group that met during the conventions of the Department of Superintendence. Walter Cocking, formerly director of curriculum, St. Louis Public Schools, at this time a professor of education at George Peabody College, chaired the group. He proposed to the officers of the National Society of Curriculum Workers that the two organizations hold a joint meeting at the 1930 convention of the Department of Superintendence in Atlantic City.

Joint meetings continued to be held the following two years, and at the 1932 conference, steps were taken to merge the two organizations. The new organization was designated as the Society for Curriculum Study. After the merger the membership was 194. From its early years the activities of the National Society of Curriculum Workers encompassed principally the holding of the annual conference, the preparation of a bibliography on curriculum planning, the publication of a list of outstanding courses of study that had been prepared by school systems and state departments, reports on curriculum planning projects in progress, reports about the professional activities of members and, beginning in 1930, the publication of a mimeographed newsletter.

After the 1932 merger, the Society began publishing its official *Curriculum Journal*. Henry Harap served as Secretary until 1938 and editor of the *Journal* throughout the life of the Society (1943). J. Paul Leonard, of Stanford University, became Executive Secretary in 1938, and Gordon Mackenzie, then at the University of Wisconsin, succeeded him in 1942. The membership in the Society reached its peak in 1939 with 807 members.

During its existence, the Society for Curriculum Study published, in addition to the *Curriculum Journal*, a number of significant and forward-looking publications. One of the most prodigious undertakings of this relatively small professional group was the publication of a monthly pictorial magazine, *Building America*, which was designed to provide interesting study material for schools to use in developing a broader curriculum of more meaning and significance to the students. It was published from 1935 to 1948 with Paul Hanna of Stanford University as leading individual in preparing and promoting the use of the magazine in schools. The study of topics with highly political significance on some issues raised bitter attacks from the radical right. In fact, the California legislature finally forbade schools to use public funds to buy the publication.

The professional books on various aspects of curriculum and instructional planning published by the Society were highly acclaimed by curriculum workers throughout the nation. Among them were *A Challenge to Secondary Education* (1935); *Integration: Its Meaning and Application* (1937); *The Changing Curriculum* (1937), a joint publication with the Department of Supervisors and Directors of Instruction; *The Community School* (1938); *Family Living and Our Schools* (1941), jointly published with the Department of Home Economics, NEA; *Americans All: Studies in Intercultural Education* (1942), sponsored with the National Council of Teachers of English and the Department of Supervisors and Directors of Instruction; *Consumer Education* (1943); and *An Evaluation of Modern Education* (1942).

Changes in Curriculum Planning and Instruction

The publications of the Society as well as those of the Department of Supervisors and Directors of Instruction illustrate the significant changes that were taking place in the 1930s in the processes of curriculum planning and development, the scope and breadth of the school curriculum, and methods and procedures of instruction.

As noted previously, a number of large and forward-looking school systems in the late 1920s had established extensive programs of curriculum construction in which a large number of committees composed of teachers and staff personnel prepared elaborate courses of study for use by teachers of the respective subject fields. But it soon became evident to supervisory and administrative staffs and to leaders in the colleges and universities that these extensive programs were not bringing about the desired improvements in the instructional programs of classrooms. Movements were initiated in the 1930s to seek primarily to affect classroom teaching rather than to prepare formal, written courses of study, per se.

The concept that learning is the result of experience, so insightfully and effectively advocated by John Dewey, was the basis for broader approaches to curriculum planning that emerged strongly in the 1930s. The publication of materials for teachers oriented to the experience concept, such as the Society's books and magazines cited and bulletins on project methods, the nature of learning, integrated units of teaching materials, and the like, expanded greatly during this period.

Primarily, plans for the direct involvement of teachers themselves in the entire planning process dominated the movement. The most notable examples of this approach to planning are the statewide curriculum planning programs of the 1930s in such states as Virginia, Kansas, and Wisconsin, and in a number of school systems. All teachers in the state or the system were invited to participate in study and discussion of curriculum issues, and then to prepare plans and materials for use in their respective classrooms.

During the same period the Progressive Education Association was carrying on the nationwide Eight-Year Study. Approximately 30 schools participated in this ongoing effort to improve the quality of the program, yet retain the academic standards associated with excellence in secondary education. The uniqueness of this study was the bringing together of the teachers who themselves would endeavor to plan and carry out instructional programs utilizing the concept of interest and experience. This is the origin of the teacher-workshop plan of inservice education, which, to this day, is so fully implemented by ASCD in its extensive programs of National Curriculum Study Institutes.

The Merger

As an outgrowth of these new approaches to curriculum planning, the two organizations primarily concerned with the quality of learning experiences took steps to bring about the merger of the Department of Supervisors and Directors of Instruction and the Society for Curriculum Study.

Sentiment for joint action and some suggestions for merger of the two organizations were evident as early as the mid-1930s. In February 1937 the two groups held a joint meeting at their respective conventions in Atlantic City. It was at this meeting that plans were formulated for the joint publication of the book *The Changing Curriculum*. There had been informal discussions among some members of the two groups about consolidation in 1936-1937. This prompted the Society for Curriculum Study to appoint a standing committee, "Committee on Consolidation with the Department of Supervisors and Directors of Instruction," which was not aggressive in taking action but was an official body to observe and study sentiment and, possibly, do a little nudging individually.

The principal factors impelling the leaders in the two organizations—the Department of Supervisors and Directors of Instruction, and the Society for Curriculum Study—to consider and work for a consolidation of efforts to influence curriculum planning and the improvement of instruction in the schools of this nation were:

1. A strong desire among the leaders to establish a strong, viable, dynamic organization within the structure of the National Education Association that would unify workers in these fields of professional activity and constitute a vehicle whereby they could exert a strong influence in the field of education comparable to that being exerted at the time by the Department of Superintendence in its field of interest.

2. Cooperation between the two organizations since 1936 in joint meetings and conferences, and in the preparation and publication of professional literature on curriculum planning and instruction.

3. The overlapping in membership, especially among leaders in education, between the two organizations.

4. The severe limitations on the scope of activities of two small organizations as contrasted to what a much larger and stronger single organization could undertake.

5. Greatly increased interest among members of the education profession in curriculum planning, teaching methods and practices, the improvement of instruction in its many aspects, and the rapidly increasing interest in educational reform in general.

Educators active in both organizations, with leadership roles in one or both groups, included Rudolph Lindquist, earlier at Ohio State University and then director of Cranbrook School at Bloomfield Hills, Michigan; Dale Zeller, Kansas State Teachers College, Emporia; Helen Heyl, New York State Department of Education; Helen Heffernan, California State Department of Education; Prudence Cutright, assistant superintendent of schools, Minneapolis; and Maycie Southall, George Peabody College.

But by far the most aggressive and influential member of both groups active in efforts to effect a merger was Hollis L. Caswell. Caswell had been on the faculty of George Peabody College since 1929 and was closely associated with Henry Harap, Walter Cocking, and Maycie Southall, all leaders in one or both groups. Caswell chaired the executive committee of the Society in 1936-1937, and from its founding in 1929 had been active in the group's work.

As early as 1935 the Department's officers had urged Caswell to accept appointment to the board of directors of the organization. The officers recognized their need for the advice and counsel, as well as the leadership, of persons who had already established themselves as scholars and dynamic movers in the work of curriculum development. Caswell served on the board from 1935 until the merger was effected. Moreover, he was elected first vice-president of the Department, 1937-1939, and hence was a member of the Executive Committee.

In addition to joint activities undertaken by the two organizations beginning in the mid-1930s, already cited, overt discussions of a merger began in 1940. Caswell wrote Harap in November 1940 that "at a recent meeting of the Executive Committee of the Department of Supervisors and Directors of Instruction Rudolph Lindquist and I discussed the whole problem of instructional leadership in the country. The idea developed that there really should be in the NEA a department that might aspire to parallel in the instructional field the American Association of School Administrators (the new name) in the administrative field. Such a department might be called the Department of Curriculum and Instruction."

Ruth Cunningham of the University of Michigan had been appointed Executive Secretary of the Department in 1940. The headquarters office had been in the NEA building since August 1936, and Cunningham was brought in to provide a new, more dynamic leadership. Cunningham, in a 1942 report to the membership, stated that "such a merger has been under consideration by the Executive Committees of the two organizations for a number of years." At a joint meeting of the two organizations at Atlantic City in February 1941, one of the principal agenda items was consideration of the proposed merger. In a report on the meeting, Cunningham wrote: "The majority of those present expressed themselves in favor of the merger, but a minority opinion was evident. Because there was a minority opposed to the action, it was decided to postpone the vote and set up committees to study the matter futher."

The two committees prepared a statement on the basis for a merger and proposed procedures. These materials were distributed to the membership, and an informal vote showed that the Department membership favored a merger by a 534 to 9 vote, and the Society by a 242 to 25 vote. The matter was formally presented to the two organizations at meetings in San Francisco in 1942. Strong opposition to the merger had developed among some of the leaders in the Department of Supervisors and Directors of Instruction, who felt that a strong system of statewide supervision of the schools would best serve the needs of the schools. They feared that a merger would result in a widespread diversion of effort through the much more informal, individual school approach strongly favored by the leaders in the Society.

The result was defeat, by a vote of 56 to 23, of a motion for the Department to approve the merger. But the membership did amend the Department's constitution so that an official vote of the membership could be held by mail. The board of directors took steps to submit to the membership a new proposal, which called for an official vote, this time on a merger. The ballots were to be returned by September 1, 1942. The membership vote strongly approved the merger.

In the meantime, the Society awaited the action by the board of the Department. Then, the culmination: the November 1942 issue of *Educational Method* and the December 1942 issue of the *Curriculum Journal* contained this official announcement:

The merger of the Department of Supervisors and Directors of Instruction of the National Education Association and the Society for Curriculum Study was approved by the joint action of the executive committees of the two organizations at a meeting in Chicago on October 10-11, 1942. This step was made possible by the vote of the members of the two organizations. A committee was appointed to work out detailed plans for the new Department of Supervision and Curriculum Development, which will hold its first meeting in St. Louis in February 1943. In the interim the two organizations will continue to function independently.

First Meeting

Because of wartime travel restrictions imposed by the federal government in February, the meeting could not be held, so the Boards of Directors of the two groups met in Chicago, 27-30 March 1943, at which time plans were formalized for the new Department, and officers were elected. These officers were: President, Ruth Henderson, supervisor of elementary education, State Board of Education, Virginia; First Vice-President, Alice Miel, Teachers College, Columbia University; Second Vice-President, Edgar M. Draper, University of Washington; Executive Secretary, Ruth Cunningham, NEA Building, Washington, D.C.

It would be acceptable to name 10-11 October 1942 or 27-30 March 1943 as the date for the founding of ASCD. Cunningham stated in her report that 1 March 1943 should be accepted as the date the Department of Supervision and Curriculum Development was established.

Wartime restrictions on travel prevented any conventions of the Department until 1946, so the work of the organization was conducted by meetings of the Board of Directors and mail votes. At a Board meeting in Cleveland on 4-6 March 1944, the following officers were elected: President, Hollis L. Caswell; First Vice-President, Ruth Henderson; Second Vice-President, Wilma G. Cheatham, Contra Costa, California, County Public Schools. New members elected to the Executive Committee were Gordon Mackenzie, then of the University of Wisconsin, and R. Lee Thomas, State Department of Tennessee; Jennie Walhert, St. Louis Public Schools, continued on the committee. At a meeting in February 1945, Caswell was reelected president. The board also voted to change the name of the organization to Association for Supervision and Curriculum Development, a Department of the National Education Association.

The first ASCD conference was held in St. Louis, 21-23 March 1946. The Board of the Association placed great emphasis on the use of committees to study and prepare plans for action on the major aspects of the supervisory process and on curriculum planning. Twenty such study committees were established, each composed of 12 members, one from each of the regional districts set up by the Board. The conference was to be an open one, with the members themselves discussing matters of concern to participants in each of the small groups scheduled throughout the convention.

There was great disdain for "spellbinders" in these early days. The conference organizers believed that since teachers are primarily the planners of learning experiences in classrooms, teachers attending an ASCD conference also should be in a position to help each other provide a quality education for children. This first general meeting was an exciting and stimulating one. (Just released from active duty in the Navy, I was one of the highly stimulated participants.)

2
ASCD and Group Process

ALICE MIEL
President, 1953-54

It is 1950. The annual conference of ASCD is being held in Denver. Gathered in a hotel parlor are 30 persons registered for a discussion group, "Supervision as Group Therapy." The leaders have invited each participant to state a problem encountered in supervising. An important principle of group therapy has been emphasized—all persons are to make their statements without fear of reprisal. Another member of the group may ask a question for clarification only; all reprimands or advice implying disapproval are to be suppressed. Later, in generalized discussion, each individual may extract privately any suggestions deemed helpful.

The descriptions of problems proceed according to plan for a time. Finally an eager supervisor can stand it no longer and slips back into a familiar pattern, advice framed as a question, "Had you thought of...?" The lesson for the group is obvious. A good laugh clears the air and the meeting proceeds.

This is one small example of a type of conference participation that caused many ASCDers in the early years to feel that an ASCD conference was not a place where you sat and listened to a speaker. You got to talk, give your own ideas, tell about your own experiences. You could hear how others had worked on the same kind of problems you had.

The Importance of Group Dynamics

Of all the ways in which ASCD has made an impact on American education, perhaps its most far reaching has been the result of its early advocacy of attention to group dynamics and its use of its own annual meeting as a training ground for practicing group procedures suitable for a democracy and therefore important to teach to the young. Not only was ASCD a pioneer in establishing a new kind of professional conference for itself; it influenced many other education organizations in the same direction.

It is understandable that the new organization resulting from the merger of the NEA's Department of Supervisors and Directors of Instruction and the Society for Curriculum Study would elect to exert its influence to advance the understandings and skills of American educators with relation to democracy. That was a time when the democracies of the new world were being threatened by fascism and people needed to know what was at stake. No one is born with the attitudes and skills needed to benefit from and contribute to life in a democracy. These are learned through the words and deeds of those around one and through living within arrangements unique to that kind of society. Democracy has to be won anew by each generation as conditions change and new problems arise. The school has a special responsibility for teaching explicitly the ways of democracy as well as creating an environment in which democratic behaviors can be practiced and analyzed. For this part of their responsibility to the young, educators need to be especially well equipped. It was fortunate that ASCD recognized this need and proceeded to fill it so well.

Interest in learning more about ways of working in groups had been aroused by the writings of a number of social psychologists in the 15-year period prior to the 1943 merger. Among those publications were H. S. Eliot's *The Process of Group Thinking*, 1928, Paul Pigor's *Leadership or Domination* and Ordway Tead's *The Art of Leadership*, both dated 1935. The NEA department had made its own contribution in the form of a bulletin, *Teachers and Cooperation*, 1937, and its eleventh yearbook, *Cooperation: Principles and Practices*, 1938.

A stream of writing in the area of group process continued during the 1940s. For example, Ronald Lippitt's experimental study of democratic and authoritarian group atmospheres was reported in 1940. *Teacher-Pupil Planning* by H. H. Giles appeared in 1941. The theme of the January 1944 issue of *Educational Leadership* was "Group Processes." Among the articles was one by Kurt Lewin on group dynamics in action.

When it came time for the Executive Committee of the Department of Supervision and Curriculum Development to decide on future yearbooks, the second one chartered was *Group Planning in Education*, 1945. *Group Processes in Supervision* was published by ASCD in 1948.

Use of Group Process in Conferences

Words of President Ruth Henderson in Volume 1, Number 1, of *Educational Leadership* foreshadowed a new approach to annual conferences:

... in the future greater emphasis will be given to developing new ways of working. People in local situations will be encouraged to experiment in new ways. . . . It is planned that programs may be reported while in process to our members, thus encouraging others to undertake similar activities and profit by the experience of the pilot group or groups. It is obvious that such an emphasis depends upon the participation of the total membership of our organization.

Only a small trail-breaking step toward wider membership participation was taken in 1946 at the first annual conference, held after restrictions necessitated by World War II had been lifted. Fifteen discussion groups were scheduled for one session of less than two hours. No competing activities were scheduled for that time slot. A chair and several discussants were named for each group. The program gave this explanation of "Group Discussions Organized Around Varied Aspects of Supervision and Curriculum Planning":

... Through ... sharing [experiences and ideas] it is believed many are enabled to move forward more effectively. In order to facilitate such sharing, group meetings have been planned. . . . in which all those attending participate in the raising of questions and sharing of experiences.

The conference of the following year was a full-fledged training exercise. The theme, "A Laboratory in Learning," was explained thus in the 1947 program:

... sessions are organized with two major purposes in mind: To provide opportunity for discussion of issues of major concern to those responsible for planning better programs of learning for children and youth.

To analyze continually the group processes at work throughout all discussions with a view toward providing experiences in an area particularly crucial to all professional effort and a hope that these experiences may stimulate more effective means of group working.

... it is believed that this meeting will not only furnish stimulation and impetus for professional growth, but will aid in the *translation of more effective means of working together in the local school situations in which we operate* [emphasis added].

Participants were given a choice of 12 groups, scheduled to meet three times for a total of over six hours. For each group, a leader, recorder, observer of group process, and several resource people were named.

The discussion group personnel, divided by function part of the time, underwent a preliminary two-hour training period conducted by Kenneth Benne, Leland Bradford, Ruth Cunningham, and Alice Miel. (Benne and Bradford were leading figures in the Bethel, Maine, summer institutes for leadership training that were attracting attention at that time.)

The first general session in this 1947 conference was designed "to point up aspects of group relationships that will serve in orienting the entire group." The assemblage was then divided into three clusters, each to hear a speaker present problems for consideration by groups under their particular umbrella topic. The announcement of group discussion to follow introductory cluster meetings read:

So far you've been on the listening end and you're ready to do some of the talking. Four discussion groups are organized under each one of the topics discussed in the period immediately preceding. Each group will work with a group leader, a recorder, an observer, and resource people. Each of these individuals has a particular function to serve in lubricating the discussion—the problems considered and the processes operative in this group. The group, however, is yours and individuals serving in special capacities are present simply as expediters. The significance of the discussion and the success of group experience will be dependent, in the main, on the group itself.

The announcement preceding the third meeting of groups, three hours in length, read in part: "You will want to pursue further questions which you raised yesterday and to open up new ones. Part of the time you will undoubtedly wish to devote to evaluation of the group processes at work."

Discussion groups had a final experience when they returned for cluster evaluation sessions:

. . . So that all may share in the processes at work in all groups, observers will take charge of these meetings for an overall evaluation of social process in each particular cluster of discussion groups.

No special help on group process was given in a conference program until 1950 when two and one-half pages were devoted to "ASCD Study-Discussion Group Procedures," prepared by J. Cecil Parker. Similar material was included in every conference program for the next six years. Such program material assumed an audience with considerable experience and sophistication in group process.

The Contributions of Discussion Groups

The last year discussion groups were scheduled in an ASCD conference program was 1969. Several observations may be made from a study of programs for the 23 years during which discussion groups played a significant role in annual conferences.

1. Discussion groups had no competition in their name slots from 1946 through 1961. In the years that followed 1961, clinics and other events were scheduled at the same time.

2. For the first three years leadership personnel were listed in the announcement of each group. Beginning in 1949 that practice was no longer followed. The reason for the change was stated in the program:

Individuals participating in the Cincinnati meeting [in 1948] were of the opinion that the problem for consideration, rather than the special personnel in each group, was the first item of importance. They recommended, therefore, that individuals with special responsibilities be listed alphabetically with no particular designation as to function.

3. Orientation of leadership personnel was provided in most years. Instructions for the orientation of group personnel showed that the team included leaders, recorders, resource people, and observers. Observers were not included after 1953. One reason for dropping the observer role may have been that some observers were accused of scolding their groups rather than assisting them in analysis of the procedures they were using. Another factor probably was that, in general, ASCD conference goers had become more knowledgeable group members in the eight years they had been having experiences with group process.

4. Conference planners experimented with different ways of organizing groups. Sometimes groups were set up within clusters, sections, or areas, each with a central topic; other times each group was an independent entity.

5. Different ways of selecting topics were tried. For instance, for two years there were three sections, one on particular research findings, a second on a designated curriculum book, and a third on promising ideas or practices.

While there were other opportunities for individual participation at an ASCD conference in the first 23 years, notably open committee meetings and annual business meetings, the discussion groups were the best laboratory for discovering the value of group procedures and for developing skill in employing them. Many of those who experienced group process at ASCD conferences (the frustrating ones as well as the highly satisfying ones) carried their enthusiasm, insights, and skills to the groups they worked with at home—pupils, future teachers, practicing teachers, graduate classes in education, or school staff planning their program.

In 1969, the last year of scheduled discussion groups, the group process skills and attitudes of the ASCD leadership and members were put to a test. ASCD met in Chicago one year after the turbulent Democratic Convention. A group of militant proponents of black concerns confronted the ASCD Executive Committee with a number of demands. Joyce Cooper, a member of the Executive Committee at the time, has furnished her version of the episode:

I went into an emergency meeting of the Executive Committee at midpoint. All of the other members were there except for the president, Muriel Crosby. Several ASCD staff members were present also.
    Everyone was tired, unhappy, and dismayed. I never had a clear story of the requests, or demands, of some for radical changes in the planned program of the conference. As I remember, they wanted a black speaker at one of the five general sessions, changed topics and changed leadership for some group meetings, and an additional or an enlarged session of the Black and White Exchange already scheduled in the program. They also wanted nonmember blacks to be admitted to the conference without paying.
    Fear was expressed by committee members that there might be chaos. Many sessions might be interrupted and disrupted. But over and over, along with the fear, there was the assurance from one and another: "ASCDers can handle it; they like to hear varied opinions." "They like to discuss; these are real problems and they are interested." "Most of our members have worked in groups; they know something about group process; they can handle most situations." "People must be allowed to talk and hear different ideas."
    This was the feeling that prevailed. The conference went on. There was no chaos.

Many who attended that conference in 1969 will remember that the Black and White Exchange turned out to be a memorable meeting. The ballroom was so packed that people even sat on the floor in groups of blacks and whites as they earnestly discussed problems of racial relationships. Perhaps no better testimony can be offered to establish the fact that ASCD reaped great benefit from all the effort invested in group process.

Is Group Process a Closed Chapter?

Assemblies, action laboratories, special sessions, and audience type events replaced discussion groups from the 1970 conference on. It may have been assumed that those attending no longer needed to work on group processes. Or it may have been assumed that group processes would continue in use through new program features. For example, when first introduced in 1964, assemblies were billed as large-group presentation-discussion meetings. Action laboratories, meeting for two and a half hours each morning for four days, were introduced thus in the 1970 program:

The purpose of the Action Laboratory is to provide for direct involvement, increased use of group process, and a way of responding directly and adequately to the interests, needs, and problems of every conferee. Emphasis will be placed upon interaction among individuals and groups, the "clash," exchange and study of ideas, and opportunities for study and direct experience in the relevant and timely problems and questions of interest to conferees.

These Action Labs, planned and conducted by large teams of specialists in each of the areas listed below, will consist of a variety of informational input activities, along with small-group and large-group discussions. They will emphasize involvement and interaction through group process techniques.

Both assumptions, that ASCDers were beyond needing help on group process and that new program features would provide experience in group process, may possibly have been valid in 1970; whether they are still valid in the mid-1980s is another question. Does the present generation of ASCD conference goers have the group process skills of a former generation? Do current ASCD conferences provide for sufficient active participation? Do assemblies and action laboratories teach needed group process skills?

Conference programs of the '80s seem heavily weighted toward presentations to a listening audience. Is group process a closed chapter for ASCD? Should it be?

3

ASCD and Supervision: The Early Years

PRUDENCE BOSTWICK
President, 1954-55

In the years before the first World War, supervisors in schools were predominantly concerned with goal setting, coordination, control, and inculcation. Under the influence of John Dewey and other who encouraged the development of democratic values and behavior in education, there came a gradual change. Attention shifted from course of study enforcement to working with teachers for the improvement of method and the quality of human relationships between teacher and child, teacher and supervisor, and supervisor and administrator. The ideal supervisor was conceived to be a person concerned with stimulating, facilitating, coordinating, and communicating.[1] Supervisors were seen as the educators who were in the most favorable professional position to exert leadership.

The Role of Supervisors and Supervision in ASCD

The study, support, and improvement of supervision in public schools has been a concern of ASCD from its very beginnings. In fact, the first survey of the membership in 1943 found that of the various people who belonged to the Association (supervisors, prin-

Author's note: I wish to acknowledge with appreciation the assistance of Elizabeth Hall Brady in designing the overall pattern of the material and in providing some essential publications for review.

[1] Adapted from Patrick Wahle's preface to a report of ASCD's Commission on Problems of Supervisors and Curriculum Workers, *Toward Professional Maturity* (Washington, D.C.: ASCD, 1967), pp. 1 and 2.

cipals, professors of education, curriculum specialists, teachers, and superintendents of schools), supervisors constituted the largest number.[2] More than other staff members, supervisors could move freely in the school situation, could work closely with both classroom teachers and school administrators, and, with sufficient opportunity, could come in contact with new ideas and promising practices.

ASCD chose to make one of its chief responsibilities the support and encouragement of the generalist in supervision, a person who, whether called supervisor, counselor, director of instruction, or whatever, is responsible for viewing the educational program as a whole and for being sure that there is balance and proper emphasis in the services and opportunities the school provides. In turn, supervisors have helped ASCD to fulfill its vital purpose of bringing to the classrooms of this country the newest and most promising ideas for the improvement of teaching materials, methods of instruction, and environment for learning.

In considering "how to bring together scholars from learned disciplines and educators in key positions to innovate change in education,"[3] ASCD determined on a program of publications as well as sponsorship of annual meetings, institutes, and workshops from which reports could be drawn. These published materials, especially *Educational Leadership* and the yearbooks, have proved to be indispensable to the work of the Association.

That the Association was able to bring together such innovators of change in education as scholars in the related fields of psychiatry, psychology, philosophy and sociology was due, in large part, to the broad base of its membership. Participants in projects and programs included not only the original ASCD membership of supervisors, curriculum workers, classroom teachers, administrators, and college professors, but also representatives of community organizations interested in improvement of programs for children and youth, as well as parents and student representatives.

At the same time that ASCD stated its purpose in relation to the study and application of new knowledge and skills, it defined a second concern, fostering the development of democratic leadership.[4] Through the publications of the Association in these early years, emphasis was placed on democratically centered procedures.

---

[2] *Educational Leadership* 1 (1944): 119.
[3] Arthur W. Combs, *The Supervisor: Agent of Change in Teaching* (Washington, D.C.: ASCD, 1966).
[4] *Educational Leadership* 1 (1944): 119.

The use of cooperative planning, the discovery of better ways to involve classroom teachers in problem identification and problem solving, the recognition of talent in a variety of persons, cooperative evaluation of educational outcomes with the use of appropriate instruments—all were present. Even as early as 1944 and 1945, yearbooks provided an analysis of styles of leadership; methods of group planning were set forth in detail. For example, the 1945 yearbook, *Group Planning in Education*, made the following suggestions:
1. Goals are such that group activity will expedite their attainment.
2. The work undertaken is relevant to goals.
3. The sequence of activities is somewhat as follows:
   a. Clarification of goals and purposes
   b. Discussion of means for attainment of goals
   c. Action in terms of means decided upon
   d. Appraisal or evaluation.
4. There is free interplay of minds at all stages of the project.
5. Consensus of opinion is striven for.

This "education for social intelligence" was illustrated with examples of teachers and supervisors planning together, as well as teacher-student planning.[5]

Study of Supervision by Supervisors

The 1946 yearbook, *Leadership through Supervision*, chaired by Lelia A. Taggart and Fred T. Wilhelms, began with a chapter by William Van Til, who explored the new educational frontiers that were opening in the nation at the end of World War II. The chapter dealt with "the culture of our times, the youth in our land, and the search for direction." To Van Til, the race between education and catastrophe did not end with World War II. He saw "education as one of the major factors operating in a society which strives desperately to achieve human control over its technology."[6] He wrote of supervisors and curriculum workers:

In the struggle to bring school instruction to bear on the significant social and individual problems of today, the supervisor and curriculum worker occupy key positions. Perhaps more than any other group serving the

---

[5] One is reminded of Dewey's definition of democratic planning: "Planning must be flexible to permit free play, to permit individuality of experience, yet firm enough to give direction to continuous development of power." From *Democracy in Education*, p. 2. (Riverside, N.J.: Free Press, 1966).

[6] Lelia A. Taggart and Fred T. Wilhelms, eds., *Leadership Through Supervision*, 1946 ASCD yearbook (Washington, D.C.: ASCD, 1946), p. 2.

schools, they are the people to whom teachers look for foresight. Since they know intimately the day-by-day workings of the classroom life, they are not so inclined toward breathtaking flights into impossible classroom Utopias as educational theorists are likely to be. Yet they are, at the same time, in a position to take a broad view of education, based upon their thinking about society, the youngsters in the schools, and the direction in which they believe education should move.[7]

A chapter by Marguerite Ransberger presented the role of the supervisor in the American scene, stressing the unique personal characteristics and the indispensable roles of those who bring to administrators and classroom teachers promising ideas from study and research in the field.

Concrete evidence of the goals, responsibilities, and problems of practicing supervisors was presented in two chapters on the responses to a questionnaire "sent during 1945 to individuals in more than two hundred and sixty communities, representing every state in the union."[8] In addition, the authors, Lelia A. Taggart and Mary C. Evans, drew material from professional literature and from an analysis of curriculum materials produced by outstanding school systems.

Findings from this extensive and impressive research were presented in excellent charts and summaries. For example, a chart in graphic form depicted the five supervisory practices rated as most promising by a selected group of 175 supervisors and principals: democratic leadership, group conferences, workshops, community relationships, and individual conferences. The graphic presentation permitted a demonstration of the differences between principals and supervisors in their judgments as to promising practices. A final chapter by Fred T. Wilhelms asked some provocative questions:

Is the supervisor merely an expert technician? Can he rely on inspiration alone? How can supervision truly fulfill its purpose? How are the opportunities for learning provided? How can all contribute to policy making? What is the distinctive role of supervision?

His response to the final question still gives today's reader insight into the point of view of ASCD as it seeks to stimulate and give direction to the practice of supervision in public schools:

Throughout this yearbook we have portrayed a supervision which is *leadership*. But we have fought at every step any smug assumption that leadership is due to a qualitative superiority of supervisors over other members of the staff. For a first requisite of good supervision is a deep

---

[7] Ibid., pp. 3-4.
[8] Ibid., p. 27.

humility and the attitude of a willing servant.

Supervision, a greatly extended supervision, is essential simply because in the organization of America's educational force it has a unique part to play. It is a role which would still be essential if every teacher in every school were already a truly superior person; only, then, it could bring its work to a tremendously increased fruition. It is a role which can be taken only by trained, professional men and woman standing just outside the classroom, yet deeply familiar with many classrooms; men and women who deal nonadministratively in warm, human relationships with many teachers. Their greatest task is to serve the teachers—and in serving them, to upbuild the schools—and the society in which they work, by removing every block, and by opening the way to the achievement of every teacher's greatest hopes and aspirations.[9]

Six years after the publication of *Leadership Through Supervision*, *Educational Leadership* devoted the entire November 1952 issue to supervision. Entitled "Supervision Says and Supervision Does," it presented a series of articles, one of which was a summary of descriptions of "Supervisors I Have Known" by teachers in a summer session class. Alexander Frazier stressed the importance of having supervisors who "think ahead" and who realize that work in instructional leadership is "never good enough." A report of a study of West Virginia's statewide program in supervision, prepared by Edwin P. Adkins and Blenda Proudfoot, recognized the great importance of cooperative work by counties, cities, colleges, and universities if supervision was to be improved.

Four Significant Areas of Research
Stimulate Supervision

Looking back on the first 20 years of ASCD's development, one is struck by the number of experiments and research projects that were undertaken in sociological and psychological fields which have bearing upon the education of children and youth. Included is Kurt Lewin's work and that of his associates in group dynamics, the work of Hilda Taba in human relations and intergroup education, Stephen M. Corey's study of action research, Daniel Prescott's research in child growth and development, and the Berkeley Growth Study under the leadership of Harold Jones. ASCD was aware of the projects and, in keeping with its aim of bringing new and promising ideas and techniques to its members, reported findings in issues of *Educational Leadership*, pamphlets, reports of institutes, and other such publications.

---

[9] Ibid., p. 122.

Group Dynamics

As early as January 1944, in the first volume of *Educational Leadership*, ASCD published an article by Kurt Lewin, entitled "The Dynamics of Group Action." Lewin asserted that early research at the Child Welfare Station of the University of Iowa supported the principle that people learn through participation in setting purposes, decision making, and in developing specific ways to attain goals.[10] In 1948, one year after the first National Training Laboratory in Group Development, in Bethel, Maine, ASCD brought to its readers an account of this effort to focus research on problems of how groups function and on methods of improving productive group life. A recorded discussion by Kenneth Benne, Leland Bradford, and Ronald Lippitt was published under the title "Toward Improved Skill in Group Living."[11] The material included discussion of role playing and sociodrama as means for the clarification of problems and issues and described the use in group process of various roles assumed by group members: leader, observer, recorder, and resource person. Adding further insight into group study was a statement by Bernard Steiner on how the results of the group discussion can be prognosticated through an analysis of what lies behind an individual's verbal expression.[12]

Additional understanding of how group processes may be used in schools was provided by a pamphlet, *Group Processes in Supervision*, prepared by the California Association of School Supervisors for publication by ASCD in 1948. Its purpose was primarily to identify practices that would improve human relationships and programs of living and learning. Instrumental in the research on the behavior of actual groups in action were six assistant superintendents, ten directors of community school projects and general county and city supervisors, two curriculum directors, and two professors of education. In addition to reports of practices, the pamphlet included articles that added special meaning and direction to this study of group processes: "Characteristics of a Democratic School" by Lavone Hanna and "Democratic Group Processes" by J. Cecil Parker and William P. Goldman, Jr.

Intergroup Relations

Another research project of importance to teachers and supervisors was that published in "Studies in Intergroup Relations."

---

[10] *Educational Leadership* 1 (January 1944): 195.
[11] *Educational Leadership* 5 (February 1948): 286.
[12] Ibid., p. 301.

Under the auspices of the American Council on Education and, later, the Center for Intergroup Education of the University of Chicago, the series described research methods, outcomes, and implications of the findings for improved interpersonal and intergroup living. Basic material for the series was derived from a study (1945-1951) entitled "Intergroup Education in Cooperating Schools" and headed by Hilda Taba. The last volume of the series, *Diagnosing Human Relations Needs*,[13] explained in detail through charts, interpretations, and analyses such resource tools as diaries, parent interviews, schedules of pupil participation, sociometric procedures, open questions, and teacher logs.

True to its aim to bring new research and new ideas to its membership, ASCD included in the 1952-53 volume of *Educational Leadership* an article by Hilda Taba, "New Tools for New Needs."[14] Further recognition of Taba's work by ASCD was the publication in this volume of an account by Maude I. Smith, a teacher, of her work at the Center for Intergroup Education in preparing a series of units.[15]

Action Research

In *Action Research to Improve School Practice*,[16] Stephen M. Corey described a way of working that permits group processes to be observed, recorded, and evaluated in terms of purposes set up by the scientific group in action. In the April 1952 issue of *Educational Leadership*, Arthur W. Foshay and Max Goodson both presented "Some Reflections on Cooperative Action Research." They sought principles of action, such as testing by reality, making values explicit, and breaking some cultural stereotypes. A more concrete description of the method at work appeared in "Action Research as a Technique for Supervision" in the May 1955 issue of *Educational Leadership*. Written by Hilda Taba and Elizabeth Noel, the article described how working groups of teachers were formed in relation to the actual problems that teachers identified. Characteristic problems were remedial help for retarded learners, methods of identifying maladjusted children, and replanning the activities program. In addition to finding important new ways of meeting problems in

---

[13] Hilda Taba, Elizabeth Hall Brady, John T. Robinson, and William Vickery, *Diagnosing Human Relations Needs* (Washington, D.C.: American Council on Education, 1951).

[14] *Educational Leadership* 10 (1953): 453.

[15] Ibid., "A Class Studies Prejudice," p. 303.

[16] Stephen M. Corey, *Action Research to Improve School Practice* (New York: Teachers College, Bureau of Publications, Columbia University, 1953).

the classroom, teachers and supervisors improved their cooperative working skills. The method of on-the-spot study of groups in action proved its effectiveness.

Growth and Development of Children and Youth

A fourth area of research that ASCD recognized as meeting criteria for scholarly studies was that concerned with child and adolescent growth and development. Findings from research in the 1930s and '40s and even extending back into the '20s, were published in the 1950s. Two studies marked by close work with teachers and parents stand out. One was carried out under the leadership of Daniel Prescott, director of the Institute for Child Study at the University of Maryland. The publication of his *Child and the Educative Process* in 1957[17] made clear the need for greater understanding of human behavior, especially of the development tasks of children and youth as they move through the school years.

A second study, the Berkeley Growth Study, directed by Harold E. Jones of the University of California, brought together a group of research scientists who studied growth from infancy to adolescence. In *Somatic Development of Adolescent Boys*,[18] Louis M. Stolz and Herbert R. Stolz present findings of their growth studies of older boys. Nancy Bayley, Mary C. Jones, and Jean Macfarlane added new information about physical growth and its relation to behavior in early childhood and middle years.

Ever concerned about growth and development, ASCD's 1952 yearbook, *Growing Up in An Anxious Age*, chaired by Ruth Cunningham, reflected the increasing desire for more knowledge about the relationship between a child's potential and his experience in the development of character and personal power. Seeking a broad base of information, the yearbook committee members chose an interdisciplinary approach. They sought ideas from educators, psychologists, psychiatrists, social anthropologists, sociologists, pediatricians, mental hygienists, economists, social workers, and guid-

---

[17] Daniel Prescott, *Child and the Educative Process* (New York: McGraw-Hill Book Company, Inc., 1957). Other volumes that emphasize the richness of this field in the 1950s include: Ruth Cunningham et al., *Understanding Group Behavior of Boys and Girls* (New York: Teachers College, Columbia University, 1951); Erik Erikson, *Childhood and Society* (New York: Norton, 1950); and Robert J. Havighurst, *Developmental Tasks and Education* (New York: Longmans, Green 1952).

[18] Lois M. Stolz and Herbert R. Stolz, *Somatic Development of Adolescent Boys* (New York: Macmillan, 1951).

ance specialists. Throughout the volume are research findings from studies of children and youth.

Yearbooks of Special Significance

Perhaps no better examples can be found of the courageous and powerful concern of ASCD for the support and spread of significant ideas and practices than in the 1962 and 1963 yearbooks: *Perceiving, Behaving, Becoming* and *New Insights and the Curriculum.*

In his introduction to *Perceiving, Behaving, Becoming,* William Van Til, then president of the Association, emphasized the timeliness of the volume, which was chaired by Arthur W. Combs:

How can it be timely in a period in which attention in education is riveted on the technological revolution, alternative proposals for organizational structures and government-favored academic areas? *Perceiving, Behaving, Becoming* is timely precisely because continuous consideration of the basic foundations of the educational program are inescapable. Regardless of what technological devices are adopted, what organization patterns prevail, what curricular content emerges, the three basic foundations of education—social, psychological and philosophical—are central in the making of the educational program.

The yearbook reflected the thinking of individuals who were working on the frontiers of psychology and education: Abraham Maslow, Carl Rogers, Arthur W. Combs, and Earl C. Kelley. They provided new ways for the teaching profession, and especially for supervisors, to see children and youth as persons with potential for becoming self-actualizing, self-fulfilling, fully functioning individuals. What the school must do is to create an appropriate learning environment to realize individual potential. That the central ideas of the yearbook found enthusiastic response in the profession and elsewhere can be seen in the continuous reprinting of the book from 1962 onward.

Although very different from the 1962 yearbook in specific content and application to educational practice, the 1963 yearbook, *New Insights and the Curriculum,* is especially stimulating for its intellectual quality and for the ideas it presents. Eminent specialists in psychology, biology, anthropology, educational sociology, and communication presented their ideas in chapters, each of which was followed by a second chapter by a member of the Association who drew implications for teaching and learning. The yearbook concentrated on potentiality, knowledge, self-management, relationships across cultures, citizenship, and creativity. Supervisors might well have been in the mind of Alexander Frazier, yearbook chair, when he urged educators to find in these readings help in asking new questions, in seeking new distinctions that have to be made, in re-examining some of the assumptions on which they have been operating, in responding more fully to what they understand very well, and in imagining new possibilities.

At the Midpoint in ASCD's History

In 1959, with increasing concern for the professionalism of educators in general supervision, the Board appointed a Commission on the Preparation of Instructional Leaders and, in 1962, a Commission on Supervision Theory. With these future-oriented proposals, ASCD moved confidently ahead. In the early 1960s, as in the early '40s, the Association stressed the need for excellence in supervision, a tradition established by the work of the preceding 20 years. Firmly held, nourished, and supported was the image of the supervisor as an agent of change who works with teachers and administrators as partner and fellow student and who is dedicated to the practice and improvement of democratic leadership.

4

ASCD and Curriculum Development: The Early Years

WILLIAM M. ALEXANDER
President, 1959-60

Curriculum development constituted at least half of the *raison d'être* as well as the title and intent of the Association for Supervision and Curriculum Development. And by and large the record is clear that in its beginnings and early years (1944-64), ASCD conscientiously and fully lived up to the promise of the merger. That is, it has served well, indeed utilized and reinforced, the interests of both supervision and curriculum development. But this integral relationship of curriculum, instruction, and supervision, and the similar concerns of teachers, curriculum directors, and supervisors makes difficult any classification of ASCD activities relating uniquely to curriculum development. Hence the basis of this chapter is the identification of specific activities from several categories that in the years before 1965 seemed most significantly and specifically related to curriculum development. The categories of activities used for this purpose are publications (yearbooks, *Educational Leadership*, booklets, and others), committees, and conferences and other related activities.

Yearbooks Focused on the Curriculum, 1944-64

The first yearbooks of ASCD followed a common practice of other organizations, including ASCD's immediate predecessors—

the inclusion of much descriptive and illustrative materials from the field. For example, Alice Miel's chapter on "How Schools Are Improved" in the 1943 yearbook of the Department of Supervisors and Directors of Instruction, *Leadership At Work* (chaired by Harold Spears), included descriptions of school program improvement from five public schools and one state teachers college; and my own chapter, "School Systems Move Ahead," included illustrations from eight school districts. Materials for such sections were usually provided by members working in these programs. These descriptive materials were regarded as useful and their dissemination through publications a helpful service to curriculum developers. The first such yearbook of the Department of Supervision and Curriculum Development on curriculum, *Toward A New Curriculum*, 1944, focused on the new educational opportunities introduced or expanded during the World War II period—for example, day care of elementary and secondary students, adult education, work experience, camping, community service, and teacher participation in curriculum development. Co-chaired by Gordon Mackenzie and J. Cecil Parker, the yearbook noted that the "method of curriculum improvement" was shifting from "the reorganization of courses and subject areas . . . to working with and for people on meaningful and vital problems, from rigidly formulated courses to plans for study developed in classrooms by teachers and pupils" (p. 4). Many illustrations of this shift were presented in subsequent chapters.

Cooperative development of a yearbook, as well as of the curriculum, was carried a step further in the 1947 yearbook, *Organizing the Elementary School for Living and Learning* (chaired by Willard E. Goslin). Four centers, each with a leader and a group of five to eight people within the area, were appointed to produce a chapter on one of the four major purposes of the elementary school defined by the yearbook chairman. Each such chapter included descriptions of practices (focused on curriculum and instruction as well as organization) in the schools of the area. Much of the content, too, was innovative, reflecting the interest of early ASCD leaders and authors in a "new" curriculum, more definitely focused on students and their present and future society.

The three yearbooks with primary curriculum focus published between 1947 and 1960 were *Action for Curriculum Improvement*, 1951 (chaired by Walter A. Anderson and William E. Young); *What Shall the High Schools Teach?*, 1956 (chaired by Arno A. Bellack and Kenneth Hovet); and *Research for Curriculum Improvement*, 1957 (chaired by Arthur W. Foshay and James A. Hall). The first of these resembled in style and structure the earlier ones annotated above;

the 1956 and 1957 yearbooks differed markedly in their inclusion of much less illustrative practice and much more theory and speculation. Thus four of the seven chapters of *Action for Curriculum Improvement* (1951) described specific practices in "Initiating Curriculum Change," "Organizing for School Improvement," "Developing Leadership," and "Evaluating Improvement Programs." Although some practices were not identified as to school and location, many were; for example, the chapter on "Developing Leadership" cited practices in ten school districts plus several statewide programs and programs of various colleges and professional organizations.

The 1956 yearbook, *What Shall the High Schools Teach?*, reflected the continuing and increasing debate over the relative importance in the high school of the disciplines and the current needs of youth and their communities. The early chapters on historical development of the problem, its current social context, and an analysis of the current status of the high school curriculum were followed by several remaining chapters that were more philosophical in nature, with the final one devoted to "Prospects in Curriculum Research."

The 1957 yearbook, *Research in Curriculum Improvement* (chaired by Arthur W. Foshay and James A. Hall), reflected the great interest of many curriculum leaders in developing and using research approaches in curriculum improvement. Following an introduction to the field by Foshay and a useful treatment of "Curriculum Research in Historical Perspective," the research process was described carefully in successive chapters on the usual steps in research, with attention also to the researcher as a person and the conduct of research in school settings. The volume was made further useful by the inclusion in its appendixes of an extensive, annotated bibliography on curriculum research and a full description of "The First Cooperative Curriculum Research Institute" (sponsored jointly in 1955 by ASCD and the Horace Mann-Lincoln Institute of School Experimentation). Thus, the 1957 yearbook represented a considerable departure from past ones in its purpose, content, and structure, and constitutes one of ASCD's major contributions to the professional literature of education.

Although not really focused on curriculum development, the 1958 yearbook, *A Look at Continuity in the School Program* (chaired by Esther J. Swenson), deserves mention here. Certainly continuity is a major aim and its lack a major problem in curriculum development. This yearbook centered attention on the problems involved in attaining continuity and on practices in organization, planning, guidance, teaching, and other efforts to improve continuity.

Three other yearbooks focused on curriculum development were published before 1965. *Leadership for Improving Instruction*, 1960 (chaired by Glen Hass), was devoted to the nature of leadership needed for improving instruction; to the expectations, roles, and responsibilities of such leaders; and to their identification, development, and appraisal. This treatment is perhaps more analytical and reflective than the 1943 and 1951 yearbooks on the same topic; perhaps, like the 1956 and 1957 yearbooks, it was therefore also regarded as less useful by some practitioners.

Balance in the Curriculum, 1961 (chaired by Paul M. Halverson), deals with the curricular balance problem that is still perplexing curriculum decision makers in the 1980s. This problem, brought into the forefront by Russia's launching of Sputnik I in October 1957, reflected the tremendous pressure on schools to train more scientists and engineers and other technicians to challenge the Russians in space. The 1961 yearbook presented a "balanced" treatment of the issues in its definition of the topic and its analysis and suggestions for dealing with it through instruction, selection of content, organization of schools, and curriculum decision making in general. Had this yearbook been more widely studied and its suggestions more widely followed, the curriculum dilemmas of the past 25 years—especially those posed by the recent report from the United States Department of Education, *A Nation at Risk*, and its aftermath—might perhaps have been lessened!

New Insights and the Curriculum, 1963 (chaired by Alexander Frazier), offered a still somewhat different yearbook purpose and structure than its predecessors on curriculum development. Its plan provided for asking "outstanding scholars to help us develop new insights and to push our thinking beyond the traditional frontiers," with each presentation of "insights" paralleled by a section written by an educator (on such topics as "Potentiality" and "Creativity") who examined the professional implications. This yearbook was a basis for reflection, discussion, and speculation rather than a guide to action or an analysis of curriculum issues for decision makers.

Thus ASCD's early yearbooks that focused on curriculum development dealt with many facets of the field and generally looked toward improvement, innovation, and change rather than to maintenance of the status quo. And they used more than one type of structure and content, varying from a well-classified and -described compilation of promising practices to a series of somewhat philosophical essays, with several in-between combinations of these approaches. The entire group provides a rich reservoir of theory and practice about curriculum issues and improvement efforts during the first two decades of ASCD.

Other Publications Focused on Curriculum Development

In addition to its journal and yearbooks, ASCD has had an extensive publications program. Although featuring a large number of relatively short publications most commonly called "booklets," the program also included the following items in the 1944-64 period: continuing series of bibliographies for several fields (especially elementary education, secondary education, and supervision and curriculum development); annual lists of outstanding curriculum materials; ASCD Conference reports; and, beginning in this period, the *News Exchange* and at least two popular leaflets, *Child Growth and Development Chart*, first noted in a 1948 report, and *One Hundred Years of Curriculum Improvement*, 1957. Today's large-scale production of audiovisual materials was a development of the later years.

The titles of booklets published by ASCD before 1965 that were focused on curriculum development reveal the wide range of interests served even in this field plus, of course, many others in supervision, teaching and teacher education, learning, growth and development, and other fields.[1] Review of the sales reported annually indicates that the 1944 booklet, *Discipline for Today's Children and Youth*, and its revisions, was by far the best seller. A series on research about teaching certain subjects, initiated in 1952 by the publication *What Does Research Say About Arithmetic?*, was quite

---

[1] Curriculum-focused booklets published before 1965 include: *Discipline for Today's Children and Youth* (1944), *Laymen Help Plan the Curriculum* (1947), *Living in the Atomic Age* (1947), *The Department Head and Instructional Improvement*, (1948), *The Three R's in the Elementary School* (1952), *What Does Research Say About Arithmetic?* (1952), *Using Free Materials in the Classroom* (1953), *School Camping* (1954), *Developing Programs for Young Adolescents* (1954), *Education for American Freedom* (1954), *Research Helps in Teaching the Language Arts* (1955), *Today's Curriculum as Seen in Representative School Systems* (1955), *Action Research: A Case Study* (1957), *Curriculum and the Elementary School Plant* (1957), *Elementary School Science: Research, Theory, and Practice* (1957), *Foreign Language Teaching in the Elementary School* (1958), *Children's Social Learning* (1958), *The High School We Need* (1959), *Education for Economic Competence* (1960), *The Junior High School We Need* (1961), *What Are the Sources of the Curriculum? A Symposium* (1962), *Using Current Curriculum Developments* (1963), *Teaching Music in the Elementary School* (1963), *Changing Curriculum Content* (1964), and *The Junior High School We Saw: One Day in the Eighth Grade* (1964).

popular, reflecting the concerns of the 1950s for answers to the critics and help to school people in improvement efforts. This interest stimulated many ASCD activities in the 1950s, several of them initiated by the Research Committee. Another series begun in this period was sponsored by the Commission on Current Curriculum Development, appointed in 1962 to represent ASCD in studying, reporting, and recommending actions relative to the national curriculum projects being stimulated by the National Defense Education Act and other federal appropriations. *Changing Curriculum Content*, a report of a conference with several project directors, and *Using Current Curriculum Developments*, were precursors of several institutes and publications on the new developments.

But the typical booklet in that list, other than those just identified, was stimulated by some problem of curriculum development or instruction in general that seemed sufficiently common to the editor and the Publications Committee (and usually with review by the Executive Committee) to justify the procurement of a manuscript. Of course, an author's proposal of a manuscript might come first, and certainly the sales prospect was an important consideration. As one of those who made extensive use of these booklets with groups and individuals in several school districts, as well as a helper in producing some materials, I can heartily applaud the ASCD booklets. The timely (but also sometimes timeless) descriptions, analyses, and suggestions found in booklets such as the following, for example, have been and may remain very helpful to school people: *Discipline for Today's Children and Youth*; *Laymen Help Plan the Curriculum*; *Action Research: A Case Study*; *The High School We Need*; and *The Junior High School We Need*. In fact, as this manuscript is being completed, I am teaching a graduate course in curriculum development once again and trying to entice my students back to some of the early ASCD yearbooks, journal articles, and booklets for a real grounding in the field!

Educational Leadership and Curriculum Development

ASCDers and many others have long regarded the official journal, *Educational Leadership*, as an excellent magazine, fully living up to the aim stated for it by the Publications Committee in its first issue, October 1943:

The hope of American education, perhaps the hope of America itself, lies in the fullest possible development and utilization of the capacity for leadership throughout its total ranks. It is to the realization of this hope that *Educational Leadership* will seek to contribute.

The journal had to move toward this lofty aim with only a part-time editor, who was also the Association's executive secretary, until October 1950, when Robert Leeper became associate editor. His leadership and assumption in time of increased responsibility for the entire publications program was undoubtedly a major factor in the contribution to education that *Educational Leadership* had made by the time of Leeper's retirement in 1978.

The journal has always devoted a major part of its space to curriculum development. More than a third (48 by the author's classification) of the issues published through May 1964 had issue themes on some topic closely related to the curriculum or some aspect thereof. Although the correspondence of included articles to the issue theme is sometimes tenuous and the coverage of the total topic frequently incomplete in *Educational Leadership*, as in other journals using issue themes, the total coverage of the curriculum field in a very few years is comprehensive.

In addition to many curriculum-focused issues plus the articles in most other issues on curriculum topics, *Educational Leadership* has provided several series of columns focused on curriculum matters. The first issue, October 1943, included four columns that would be continued in some form for many years, and two of them were directly related to curriculum development: "The New—In Review," by Alice Miel, included reviews and notices of books, films, recordings, and other developments. "Tools for Learning," by I. Keith Tyler as first contributor, with others to follow on various groupings of learning aids; "Front Line in Education," by Henry Harap, and "The Importance of People," by Stephen M. Corey, were news reviews and general commentaries. "The New—In Review" was later broken into various columns appearing under one or more of these titles for a few years each: "Curriculum News," "Curriculum News and Bulletins," "News and Trends," "Significant Books in Review," and "Curriculum Developments." The Association's interest in curriculum research was manifested by a column of that name first appearing in October 1949 and continuing, with occasional lapses, through the early period (1944-64). All of these efforts, and a few other columns of shorter duration or with other foci, attested to the interest of the organization in providing its membership with updated news, notices, and events of importance in curriculum development. Such columns ("Reviews" and "Trends") continue today.

ASCD Committee Activities and
Curriculum Development

ASCD has long worked for its major goals, including the facilitation of curriculum development, through small groups, variously called over the years "boards," "committees," "commissions," and "councils," appointed for particular assignments. Twelve such groups are known to have been at work on curriculum matters during some portion of ASCD's early years. I have not been able to search out the exact times of these committees' appointments and terminations nor all of their activities since the chief records consulted (Executive Committee minutes, 1950-64) dealt primarily with committee recommendations and related Executive Committee actions. These references and my own recollections about some committees constitute the major source for identifying committee activities during ASCD's early years.

Committees frequently planned and held, in conjunction with the ASCD staff, conferences or institutes related to committee goals. The Research Board was the first committee to recommend and conduct—in cooperation with the national staff and with the Horace Mann-Lincoln Institute of School Experimentation—conferences or institutes to stimulate interest or otherwise assist in developing activities devoted to the group's special focus, in this case, that of curriculum research. The first such institutes were held in 1951 and 1952 and, as related by Jack Frymier in Chapter 7 of this book, several others were held in ensuing years. Other groups recommending and, in some cases, conducting special conferences or institutes during the early years were those on International Understanding (March 1954),[2] Elementary Curriculum (May 1961), and Current Curriculum Developments (May 1963).

The most frequent recommendations of the committees have to do with publications—their preparation by the committees or others in the form of yearbooks, booklets, or articles. Entire series of publications were sponsored by the Research Committee and the Current Curriculum Developments Committee, with many items actually written by committee members. In addition, the following committees apparently gave much consideration to publications: International Understanding (March 1954), Preparation of Core Teachers (March 1955), Education of Adolescents (March 1958), Ed-

---

[2] The dates given after committees are those of Executive Committee meeting minutes in which the committee's particular activities are first mentioned.

ucation for Economic Competence (March 1960), Elementary Curriculum (March 1960), Secondary Curriculum (October 1960), and General Education (May 1961). The preparation of working or position papers was also recommended and, in some instances, used for stimulation of further activities: International Understanding (May 1961), and Secondary Curriculum (October 1963).

The committees' activities and recommendations for other groups frequently included planning special programs for the annual conference. Cooperation with other professional associations was recommended by International Understanding (October 1956), Research (April 1958), and Current Curriculum Developments (October 1960), and some beginnings were made through joint publications. Cooperation and joint sponsorship were recommended by several groups, e.g., Economic Education (March 1954), Research (March 1954), Core Teaching (October 1958), and Cooperative Action for Curriculum Improvement (March 1960).

Of course, much time of the early committee meetings of ASCD, as well as the later ones and in other organizations, was spent in analyzing, discussing, sharing, and even arguing positions, solutions, issues. Our ASCD committees constituted major working groups of the national organization during the early years, and they influenced greatly our stance, direction, and movement. The subsequent expansion and recognition of ASCD should surely be credited in considerable part to the discussions and activities of these committees and their members, and the larger membership influenced by their discussions and consequent conferences and institutes, publications, collaborations, and special projects.

ASCD's Other Activities for Curriculum Development

Certain other ASCD activities having curriculum relationships should at least be mentioned. First of all, the Annual Conference of the first two decades gave priority to various types of programs dealing with curriculum developments and issues. Examination of many of the printed programs for these years reveals these types of sessions on curriculum:

- General Session addresses on curriculum issues and goals
- Study Groups on a variety of curriculum topics: curriculum areas, core curriculum, curriculum planning and development, curriculum balance, curriculum research, evaluation, resources, etc.
- Assemblies (speakers, panels) on topics similar to those listed for Study Groups
- Clinics, demonstrations, job-alike sessions—problem-

centered—for curriculum directors (and other special groups).

The adoption of resolutions at the Annual Conference generally included further debate or opportunity for debate on issues frequently related to curriculum development. The chief effect of some resolutions might be simply the improved morale of those proposing them, but many directed an action by some officer or group of the Association.

Earlier I mentioned special conferences and institutes related to curriculum development. During the early years of ASCD, these activities were generally extensions of the program of national committees. The curriculum-relevant activities of state or regional units that I knew about during the 1944-64 period related primarily to committees and conferences. National committees sometimes carried on correspondence with affiliate units, and some activities of national committees such as institutes and publications were reflected in or paralleled by affiliates' committees. National committee representatives occasionally spoke at conferences of the local units in the early years, and regional meetings during national conferences were frequently devoted to national committee concerns.

ASCD's Role in Curriculum Development

This review has confirmed my belief that ASCD rendered a major contribution to curriculum development during its first two decades. It provided a forum for debate on curriculum issues, a resource center for sharing curriculum developments, and a stimulus to curriculum improvement. ASCD stood for the forward-looking in curriculum during its early years, and I hope and expect that this influence will help to make permanent its tilt toward curriculum improvement and diversity rather than toward maintenance and uniformity.

5

ASCD and Social Forces

WILLIAM VAN TIL
President, 1961-62

International Affairs

International relations and international education were among the earliest social concerns of the organization born during World War II and named ASCD in 1946, the heady postwar year in which the United Nations first met. The young ASCD was willing to deal with controversial issues in world affairs. A synthesis of resolutions for 1947-1967[1] reports:

In a world without effective world government, destruction constantly threatens mankind [1950]. War is not inevitable, and peace building is and must be a major concern of educators in a free society. While we recognize the necessity of, and vigorously support, a national policy of military strength, we recommend a parallel development of a positive, cooperative, and massive effort to build for peace. We urge a still greater effort on the part of our Nation to join with other free nations in developing their economic resources and human potential [1951; Synthesis 1947-1967].

Recommended actions in 1950 included calls for "an assembly of nations . . . to bring about an effective government of the world" and for "a national conference . . . [on] the world crisis." The United Nations was commended in 1951 for its efforts to find peaceful so-

---

Author's note: I acknowledge with appreciation Phil C. Robinson's review of the section on human and civil rights.

[1] This chapter draws on annual listings of resolutions and on four syntheses of resolutions prepared by ASCD committees: *Beliefs, Resolutions and Positions of ASCD, 1947-1967; Synthesis of ASCD Resolutions 1978; Synthesis of ASCD Resolutions Through 1980; Synthesis of ASCD Resolutions Through 1984.* When an annual listing of resolutions is used as a source, the year is cited. When a synthesis is used as a source, the year(s) of the resolution and specific synthesis are cited in brackets.

lutions to problems, and educators were urged to "give added emphasis to the purposes and achievement, as well as the problems of the UN." A 1954 resolution called for "a free atmosphere in which children and youth may learn about the United Nations and its agencies."

Resolutions throughout the 1950s proposed that "every teacher, supervisor, and administrator should strive to strengthen education in international relations . . . and help all learners understand and practice democracy in a world context" [1958; Synthesis 1947-1967].

Whether titled international understanding, or international cooperation and education, or world cooperation and education, committees/commissions worked from ASCD's early years into the mid-1970s for the "preservation of freedom and democracy within a humane world community" [1961, Synthesis 1947-1976]. One notable achievement was the sponsorship of a world conference in 1970 to deal with worldwide problems of curriculum development and supervision of instruction. This conference, held at Asilomar, California, was planned by the Commission on International Cooperation in Education, co-chaired by Alice Miel and Louise Berman. Four years of planning culminated in sessions that brought together 303 educators from 53 nations for a ten-day working conference. The conference was followed by the formation, with ASCD help, of the World Conference for Curriculum and Instruction, which became an active, independent organization for intercultural communication in multicultural settings.

In 1969, during the involvement of the United States in the quagmire of Vietnam, a yearbook was commissioned on issues of war and peace and on teaching about peace. Under the editorship of George Henderson, *Education for Peace: Focus on Mankind*, was published in 1973.

Recently, ASCD resolutions have included in 1979 endorsement and cooperation with the International Year of the Child. Support for the nuclear freeze proposal was expressed and conveyed to governmental leaders in 1983. In 1985 an ASCD resolution called "on the national administration and the U.S. Congress to negotiate arms control and arms reduction agreements with the Soviet Union and among the nations. ASCD calls on educators to accelerate school programs to help young people discuss and understand problems of arms control and arms reduction in the nuclear age." In 1985 ASCD affirmed "its commitment to foster the type of education and goodwill that safeguards the ideas of peace, freedom, and human dignity." The resolution urged "affiliate groups and members to implement . . . this commitment" and "to develop, advocate, and teach methods for resolving individual and group conflict through nonviolent means."

ASCD has not had a commission on international cooperation since the mid-1970s. Perhaps a renaissance of ASCD activity as to international cooperation and peace education is in the offing as the threat of nuclear catastrophe grows.

McCarthyism and Censorship

The first major text of willingness of the young ASCD to respond to and attempt to counter malignant social forces came in the late 1940s and early 1950s during the era of McCarthyism, named for the tactics of Senator Joseph McCarthy. Political McCarthyism at the national political level was accompanied by educational McCarthyism largely on the local community level. ASCD reacted swiftly to educational McCarthyism fostered by political-economic forces and patrioteers. In the late 1940s the organization set forth its views on censorship:

An important function of the school in a democratic society is to guide children and youth according to their maturity levels in intelligent, socially constructive, and moral action by developing their powers of critical intelligence. Successful performance of this function requires freedom for teachers and students to explore ideas through access to all media of communication. Attempts, either overt or subtle, to censor currently unpopular expressions of ideas or to prevent examination of controversial issues of classrooms hinders the development of the power of critical discrimination and tends to establish a coercive concept of Americanism" [1949; Synthesis 1947-1967].

The resolution then named and condemned specific acts of censorship.

While some education organizations remained timidly silent, columns and articles in *Educational Leadership*, as well as conference speakers, took up the problem. A distillation of resolutions, 1947-1963, summarizes several ASCD resolutions adopted during the era of McCarthyism.

It is clear, however, that certain organized groups both of the left and right, seek to undermine, weaken, and destroy our public schools by unfounded criticism of individuals and of educational organizations, by campaigning to weaken the financial support needed by the schools, by seeking to censor textbooks and other materials used for instructional purposes in the schools, and by otherwise attempting to block the development of sound educational programs.

William H. Burton of Harvard University urged the ASCD board and executive committee to develop a yearbook on the irresponsible attacks on school systems and educational leaders. When Burton fell ill, literally a casualty of the struggle for freedom of the mind, I was asked to take over the editorship of the 1953 yearbook. *Forces Affecting American Education* carried chapters by Harold Benjamin, Willard E. Goslin, President Charles S. Johnson of Fisk University, myself, and Robert Skaife of the Commission for the Defense of Democracy who described local conflicts and named unfair individuals and groups. The yearbook became the target of national spokesmen for reaction. Executive Secretary George Denemark mounted a vigorous defense in behalf of the affirmation of democratic values that characterized the yearbook.

Since the conclusion of ASCD's 1982 Project on Censorship and the Curriculum, ASCD has been active in the National Coalition Against Censorship. Though no commission on censorship presently exists, ASCD has continued to be vigilant in such areas as support for academic freedom and opposition to censorship and dangerous groups, as recent resolutions demonstrate:

The ASCD recognizes the great danger opposed by groups like the KKK, the American Nazi Party, and ROAR (Restore Our Alienated Rights). ASCD should disseminate this concern through communication channels of the organization [1976].

ASCD recognizes that censorship limits students' access to information. Such action reduces the range of information available to students and violates their right to explore ideas.

ASCD should specifically state its opposition to censorship and encourage its membership to take those actions necessary to ensure students free access to information, to provide open exploration of alternative views, and to foster freedom of thought [1982; Synthesis 1984].

Human and Civil Rights

Another area in which ASCD has been outspoken and active is the field of human and civil rights. Well before the Supreme Court decision on public school desegregation, ASCD passed resolutions against racism and in support of civil rights [1947, 1948, 1950, 1952, 1954]. After the 1954 decision, resolutions supportive of desegregation were promptly adopted:

The decision of May 17, 1954, by the Supreme Court of the United States regarding the illegality of the principle of segregated schools was right and just. We pledge our efforts to develop respect for and implementation of the decision [1955]. Furthermore, every teacher, supervisor, and administrator at every level of education should dedicate his efforts to the development of the concept of the brotherhood of man, to confirmation of the inalienable rights with which we are endowed [1956], and to improvement of community relations in regard to Americans of varied nationality backgrounds, races, religions, and social economic status [1957].

Resolutions updating ASCD's stance on human and civil rights and specifying opposition to attempts to evade the decision were adopted regularly throughout the 1950s and thereafter. As ASCD said in a 1970 resolution:

ASCD has consistently asserted the critical importance of education in creating respect for human and civil rights in America. Since 1947, eighteen resolutions have been passed by ASCD which support this point of view.

Nevertheless, as events of the past decade attest, the scourge of racism in both subtle and blatant form still persists in American society. ASCD reaffirms its position that the achievement of full integration of minority groups into every facet of American life is a major task of education. We recommend that:

1. ASCD oppose, in every way possible, the use of public funds for the support of private schools organized to maintain racial segregation.

2. ASCD voice opposition to black separatism and any other form of separatism as a solution to the problem of racism. ASCD voices opposition to white racism and any other form of racism.

3. ASCD, in the extension of integration, support the conscientious utilization of professional competence in leadership positions in education and, indeed, in American life as a whole, regardless of race, creed, or class.

Nor were the problems of other minorities overlooked. ASCD supported the Native American and the Latino Caucuses by "(1) encouraging increased participation in ASCD program planning and membership on the staff, (2) providing educational programs on cultural pluralism, and (3) endorsing educational legislation pertaining to these two groups" [Synthesis 1984]. The organization has supported education for the children of illegal immigrants, resolving in 1978 that "while illegal immigrants in this country have violated immigration laws, their children have not, and should not be subjected to a denial of schooling privileges" [1978; Synthesis 1984].

As a corollary to positions on human and civil rights, ASCD has long supported programs of human relations education. When what formerly was called intergroup and intercultural or human relations education was more often called multicultural and multiethnic education in the mid-1970s, ASCD reaffirmed its support, saying in a 1983 resolution: "ASCD supports desegregation and integration, equal educational opportunity, affirmative action programs, and multicultural and multiethnic education."

ASCD has practiced what it preached in the area of human and civil rights. Membership in the national organization has always been open to people of all races, religions, and national backgrounds. But in the early years of ASCD, some units in southern states were segregated in practice. Solution of the problem prior to national civil rights legislation was difficult since southern educators, however personally sympathetic they might be to desegregation, frequently encountered state laws mandating segregation and always encountered power structures supporting racism. In the 1940s and '50s, the national governing boards of ASCD pressed steadily for the establishment everywhere of desegregation as a practice in state units; in time, integrated state affiliates in all regions came about.

In chapter 6 of this book, Phil C. Robinson describes the current roles of blacks and other minority group members in ASCD.

Positions on Issues of the 1960s and 1970s

Throughout John F. Kennedy's New Frontier program and Lyndon B. Johnson's Great Society program, ASCD continued to respond to social realities. ASCD repeatedly supported federal aid for education. This was not a new departure for ASCD, for the organization had favored federal aid to public schools since 1948. ASCD held that federal financial support to American schools, without federal control, was essential and that such support should encompass the total educational program.

One tactic employed by opponents of school segregation was to penalize black educators by not absorbing them into the staff of newly desegregated schools. ASCD's many resolutions favoring educator employment without regard to race date back to 1947 and were stepped up as the problem of fairness to black educators became critical in the 1960s.

A Great Society initiative supported by ASCD was emphasis on problems of urban education. A commission on urban education was instituted by ASCD during the late 1960s. National conferences stressed approaches to urban difficulties. A 1981 resolution pointed out "the need to exchange information and discuss issues relating to urban schools"; it asked ASCD to "disseminate information on proposals for improving the quality of urban education, on approaches for developing realistic funding for programs, and on the improvement of public perception of urban schooling."

The Ferment of the 1970s

The late 1960s and early '70s were times of continuing social turmoil. In addition to the civil rights crusade, America experienced protests against the Vietnam War and saw the emergence of a new phase in the movement for women's rights. The activities of ASCD were affected.

The 1969 ASCD conference in Chicago experienced confrontation tactics by militant white and black proponents of black concerns. The 1970 conference in San Francisco saw the emergence of a radical caucus that met at conferences until its demise a few years later. Proponents of equity in the field of women's rights fostered several proposals that were usually adopted as ASCD policy. For instance, the Equal Rights Amendment was endorsed [1972, 1973, 1978; Synthesis 1978]. In 1974, a long resolution set forth 20 criteria for evaluating the treatment of minority groups and women in textbooks and other learning materials.

ASCD reflected the ferment of the 1970s. Commissions, later titled working groups of the organization, included black concerns, a group on ethnic bias in preparation and use of instructional materials, an oppressive practices study, and training programs for implementation of shared power. Yearbooks of the 1970s were more socially oriented than many of their predecessors. They included *To Nurture Humaneness* (1970); *Freedom, Bureaucracy, and Schooling* (1971); *Education for Peace* (1973); *Education for an Open Society* (1974); and *Schools in Search of Meaning* (1975).

Separation of Church and State

Church and state relationships were a continuing focus of ASCD concerns. In 1952 the organization supported "the fostering of moral and spiritual values as an integral part of an effective public school program." In 1954, ASCD expanded on this view.

Fostering moral and spiritual values is an integral part of an effective school program. ASCD encourages the development of classroom procedures that continue to safeguard the rights of individual conscience in matters of religious belief when discussing religious institutions and their contributions to American civilization. Parents and religious educators are encouraged to meet these religious needs which may not be met in public school classrooms [1954; Synthesis 1980].

In 1970 ASCD said:

The Constitution and the traditions of the United States support separation of church and state. At a time when public funds for education are inadequate, ASCD opposes public funds being used to support parochial education [1970; Synthesis 1978, 1980].

In 1981 ASCD went on record against voucher proposals. A 1981 resolution also opposed tuition tax credits. In 1984, ASCD opposed prayer in public schools:

The long established tradition of separation of church and state guaranteed by the First Amendment has served the American people well.

Therefore, ASCD opposes proposals for legislation or constitutional amendment that authorize prescribed mandated prayer or religious meditation programs in public schools and which could contribute to conflicts among people of good will who differ in their religious observances. Prayer and meditation are the responsibility of family and religious institutions.

Government Policies of the 1980s

Several recent resolutions have been critical of recent trends in government. After the defeat of the ERA, ASCD in 1983 advocated that "members should become acquainted with the positions taken on the equal rights issue by legislators in their states and take such positions into account when voting in subsequent elections. ASCD also urges Congress to renew past support for an equal rights amendment and urges supporters of equal rights to develop further approaches to achieve their goals."

Two 1983 resolutions called on "government leaders of the nation to reorder current priorities so as to recognize that education is fundamental to the public interest" and "to restore the achievement of democratic human relationships in culturally pluralistic America to a high priority." The latter resolution pointed out that "the advancement of better human relations among Americans of diverse backgrounds is threatened by indifference and neglect and also by the instigation of reversals of forward-looking policies by some federal and state governmental agencies."

In 1984, following publication of a spate of reports calling for reform in education, ASCD pointed out that some national reports "have failed to address the issues of educational equity, including race, culture, economics, and sex" and called for the Department of Education to commission a national study of desegregation and integration implementation. Calling for increased investment in education, a resolution pointed out that "American education has not been given high financial priority on the national agenda. Indeed, in recent years, education has experienced severe funding cuts in many programs. The implementation of many recommendations for the improvement of educational programs will require an increase in financial support from federal sources as well as from state and local revenues."

In 1985 ASCD returned to the issue of meeting health and education needs:

ASCD calls on the President and Congress to recognize that our children and youth are a powerful resource of this nation. The greatest defense of our freedom is a healthy, educated population. The health and education needs of our society must be accorded the same priority as our defense systems as conventionally defined. Today's federal financial deficit must be decreased but not to the detriment of the health and education needs of our children.

ASCD and Social Issues

ASCD, over a period of more than 40 years, has taken positions on controversial issues in society and schools. It has *supported* social forces that foster the historic American democratic values and support democratic education. It has also *opposed* social forces—those that would lead to war; institute censorship and stifle the use of intelligence; deny human and civil rights; impede government from doing for its people collectively what they cannot do for themselves individually; discriminate against women, blacks, and minority ethnic groups; break down walls of separation of church and state; and penalize children and youth for the failure of adults.

6

ASCD and Ethnic Groups

PHIL C. ROBINSON
President, 1984-85

The history of ASCD strongly reflects a commitment to the inclusion of all racial minorities and various ethnic groups. Evidence of black participation in ASCD's national programs can be traced to the organization's beginnings. ASCD passed resolutions in 1967, 1969, 1975, and 1977, which expressed, in various ways, the commitment of the Association to minority involvement and participation.

Involvement at the State Level

A 1983 national resolution focused on the stubborn problem of broadening minority representation at the affiliate leadership levels in the states. Today it is encouraging to report the sharp increase in minority participation in ASCD at the state and commonwealth level. Of special significance is the fact that 18 people of minority group backgrounds have served as affiliate presidents since 1981. Of those, 12 are black, four Hispanic, and two Asian.

Among the affiliates, the state of Michigan has led the way in demonstrating affirmative strategies for accomplishing minority group representation within the leadership ranks. For example, Michigan's nominating committee has implemented a plan to assure the election of members of a minority to key positions by developing a slate of qualified minority background candidates for any given office. In addition, Michigan has written into its constitution stipulations that there be minority representaton on its

Author's note: I wish to acknowledge with appreciation the advice of Elizabeth Randolph and Alvin D. Loving, Sr., in preparing this chapter.

Board of Directors. This mandate is fulfilled through election or by appointment by the president.

The opportunity to participate at the affiliate level provides access for minority group leaders to recognition within the national ASCD community. Michigan has elected five blacks as ASCD state presidents: Donna Carter, LaBarbara Gragg, Jim House, Chuck King, and myself. Two of Michigan's black educators, Alvin D. Loving and I, went on to become national ASCD presidents.

Participation at the National Level

At the national level, participation by minority group members in the annual conference has long been evident and has increased during the 1970s and 1980s. At its annual conferences, ASCD has consistently scheduled three or four nationally known speakers at the general sessions. Blacks and Latinos have long been among those so involved. A sampling of minority group spokespersons includes: the Rev. James H. Robinson, Church of the Master; Jaime Benitez, University of Puerto Rico Chancellor; Lerone Bennett, Jr., *Ebony* magazine managing editor; Julian Bond, Georgia legislator; Benjamin E. Mays, president, Morehouse College; Phillip V. Sanchez, ambassador to Honduras; and Jerry Apodaca, governor of New Mexico. Others were Kenneth B. Clark, whose research helped bring the Supreme Court decision on school desegregation (*Brown vs. Board of Education*); Shirley Chisholm, former congresswoman; and Benjamin Hooks, president, National Association for the Advancement of Colored People.

National ASCD conferences have also provided an arena for prominent educators from minority-group backgrounds to share their views on ways to improve the quality of education. Among the conference speakers were A. Donald Bourjeois, St. Louis Model City Agency; Ruth Love Holloway, Right to Read Program; Barbara Sizemore, USOE; James E. Comer, Yale Child Study Center; Uvaldo Palomares, "Quality through Diversity"; and Superintendents J. L. Jones of Miami, Florida, and Arthur Jefferson of Detroit, Michigan.

The term "pluralistic society" commonly occurs in ASCD publications and resolutions statements. Such concern for broad representation of issues and problems was reflected in the establishment of working groups on "Black Concerns," "Native Americans," and "Latino Concerns." These ASCD working groups have provided a public forum for minorities and other members to focus on solutions to problems as well as strategies to improve levels of minority participation. Their findings and recommendations have been expressed to the Executive Council, the Board of Directors, and officers through memoranda and resolutions proposed for adoption.

The richness and resourcefulness of ASCD as a viable organization is due, in part, to the leadership and challenge of its multi-ethnic membership. At the national level, organizational leadership opportunities for people from minority group backgrounds have grown. As early as 1965, ASCD took steps to have minority representation on the Executive Council; a black man was appointed to a one-year unexpired term on the Executive Council. Since 1971, at least two to four people of minority ethnic backgrounds have served on the Executive Council each year.

Roles in National Leadership

Authorized by the governing bodies, Jim House chaired a special membership committee, appointed in 1968, to increase ASCD minority membership. This work continued through 1971 and was somewhat successful in meeting its goals. In 1971, "Education of Black Children and Youth" was identified by the Black Concerns Council as the crucial issue of the day. One hundred fifty-three members of the Council attended the 1971 St. Louis ASCD conference.

After the Kerner Report was released, Alvin D. Loving, Sr., became ASCD's first black national president (1971-72). His conference theme was "From Kerner to the Year 2000—Action for the '70s." The Kerner Commission's report in the late 1960s was called an "honest beginning" on improvement of race relations in America. At the time of the conference focus on the Kerner findings and recommendations, there was evidence that the nation was racially polarized and in critical need of leadership from professional educators. The conference called upon ASCDers to rise to action on an unprecedented scale to shape a future compatible with the historic ideals of American society.

During the 1970s, publications by blacks and other minorities through the journal, pamphlets, and yearbooks dramatically increased. For instance, in 1974, for the first time black authors outnumbered white authors as contributors to an ASCD yearbook, *Education for an Open Society*, chaired jointly by Delmo Della-Dora and Jim House.

When controversial issues arose, such as busing to achieve school integration, ASCD did not hesitate to take a stand, even though the Association's decisions were sometimes unpopular. In 1976, outgoing president Delmo Della-Dora was commended through an ASCD resolution, which read, in part:

ASCD commends outgoing President Delmo Della-Dora for his support of busing and testimony before a Congressional Committee. . . .

ASCD wishes to inform the Executive Council and officers of its support for continued vigorous expansion of busing programs as a necessary step toward equitable, quality and integrated education . . . and to instruct the Council and officers to seek ways to actively support such busing programs.

The election of the next black ASCD national president was the result of uncommon courage by the national Nominating Committee. Three black women were nominated, assuring that one would be elected. This resulted in the election of Elizabeth S. Randolph of North Carolina (1977-78).

During Randolph's presidency, the first ASCD Five-Year Plan came into being. At the October 1977 meeting, President Randolph opened the Executive Council session and challenged the Council to begin long-range planning. She recalled for the group that the Executive Council members had decided to assume this leadership responsibility themselves, in response to the Review Council's recommendation that a long-range effort be undertaken to set directions for the Association.

The Year of the Teacher

In 1984, I became ASCD's third black president. I was the first practicing principal, white or black, so elected. The Five-Year Plan was then well-established, and I attempted an ambitious broad-ranging program for ASCD. The drive to have 1985 celebrated as the "Year of the Teacher" resulted in many "firsts" for ASCD.

Senate Joint Resolution 48, naming 1985 the Year of the Teacher, was introduced by Senator Carl Levin (D., Michigan) and passed by the U.S. Senate. The companion House Joint Resolution 151, introduced by Congressman William D. Ford (D., Michigan), had received 132 co-sponsors at the time of this writing. In addition, every governor heard about ASCD and its commitment to building a strong educational system throughout the nation. State affiliate presidents and their respective networks of political contacts appealed to governors for support of the Year of the Teacher project. Thirty-five governors issued executive proclamations in support of this unique recognition of teachers. Many state boards of education followed their governor's lead by issuing supporting board resolutions. Twenty-five national organizations also endorsed the Year of the Teacher concept; their names are listed in the December 1984 issue of *Educational Leadership*.

The Year of the Teacher promotional campaign I developed was intended to give public visibility to the contribution of teachers, and to ASCD's forward thinking as an association. Drawing on the ingenious talents of Al Way, ASCD's graphic artist (also a black man), the Association developed a theme logo, which depicted children of different races looking eagerly toward their teacher. The figures within the logo design certainly captured the essence of a positive, multiethnic exchange. This same logo has found its way onto state and local ASCD conferences and workshop programs, public relations brochures sponsored by education groups, and other publications. ASCD also commissioned the production of T-shirts, tote bags, and lapel pins with the Year of the Teacher logo. Public service announcements were aired on television.

The staff of ASCD played a major role in carrying out the implementation plans for the Year of the Teacher project. Special credit is due to Executive Director Gordon Cawelti, Associate Director Jean Hall, Associate Director Diane Berreth, Executive Editor Ron Brandt, and Conference Coordinator Sarah Arlington for their creative leadership and support of this national thrust. The 1985 conference title, "Exalting Teaching and Learning," reenforced the major elements of the yearlong theme.

Recognizing that improving the image of teaching as a profession begins with attracting competent and dedicated young people to become teachers, ASCD contacted more than 700 deans of the nation's schools of education for assistance. My correspondence to them in 1985 expressed ASCD's concern about improving the image of the teaching profession, remedying the imminent teacher shortage, and expanding efforts to recruit capable persons to enter the teaching profession. University faculties and other concerned educators were urged to tell the story of how teaching can provide a challenging and stimulating outlet for those with creative energies and a love for children.

A Continuing Goal

ASCD is a rich organization serving diverse populations. Recognizing the wealth of resources and positive contributions to be made by a multiethnic leadership and multiethnic membership must be a primary goal that is continually sought. It can only be reached if we work unremittingly toward this end at the national and state affiliate levels.

7

ASCD and Research

JACK FRYMIER
President, 1972-73

Historically, the members of the Association for Supervision and Curriculum Development have reflected an interest in and a commitment to research. As a way of comprehending and coping with both the possibilities and problems inherent in supervision and curriculum development, research has been regularly incorporated into the structure and function of ASCD.

Always an issue, the questions related to research have been: Should ASCD encourage, use, support, sponsor, conduct, or disseminate research? Or should the organization do all of these things? Over the years, different answers to these questions have resulted in changing emphases with varying results at different points in time.

At least three different types of activity have been evident within ASCD: committee work, special institutes or programs, and publications of various kinds.

Committee Work

Committees are the lifeblood of an organization. Such groups plan, accomplish, and evaluate the ongoing activities of the organization, breathing vitality and vigor into the purposes and projects to which the organization is committed. And committee members always evidence their own personal beliefs, experiences, and skills in accomplishing their responsibilities.

The membership of ASCD Research Committees over the years

Author's Note: I wish to acknowledge with appreciation Alexander Frazier's and Phil Hosford's reviews of this chapter.

reads like a "Who's Who" in American education, which includes, among others:

Hollis Caswell	Hilda Taba	Alexander Frazier
William Alexander	Laura Zirbes	James Raths
Lawrence Haskew	Stephen Corey	Fred Rogers
Arthur Jersild	David Russell	Virgil Herrick
Ruth Cunningham	Max Goodson	James Macdonald
William Bristow	Robert Bills	Harry Passow

In addition, the Research Committees repeatedly requested the Executive Committee to employ a staff member whose primary responsibility would be to emphasize research and nurture research throughout the organization. Robert Fleming was asked to work part-time for ASCD while he was at the University of Tennessee, for example, and Bernard Everett was sought for part-time work from his position in the public schools of Massachusetts. Other people were asked to perform special roles at other times.

In this way, proposals were written, conferences were conducted, relationships were established, materials were published, and ASCD monies were spent, always furthering the purposes of ASCD as an organization and the purposes of people such as those described above.

A careful study of the minutes of Executive Committee meetings makes it apparent that the ASCD Research Committees have struggled throughout the decades to develop ways of working that would be theoretically defensible and practically effective. It was decided early on, for example, that ASCD would not do research, per se, but would work instead to create conditions in which school districts could work collaboratively with interested parties to generate appropriate answers to the vexing questions that routinely arise in schools. Subsequent committees tended to adhere to that policy position.

On more than one occasion, funds were requested from outside funding agencies to support activities of the Research Committee, but these efforts generally failed to generate material support. However, the process of preparing the proposals and incurring commitments frequently led to modified versions of the proposed projects being accomplished through cooperative ventures with other organizations or institutions. For example, ASCD and the Horace Mann-Lincoln Institute of School Experimentation at Teachers College, Columbia University, jointly sponsored a series of research institutes in the early years. In other instances, the national ASCD worked directly with state ASCD affiliates to produce research-oriented materials for publication and dissemination.

The talents, orientations, creative abilities, and motivations of people such as those listed above brought research into the day-to-day lives of many ASCD members over the years. The organization has been fortunate to be able to tap and utilize the energies and insights of such persons for the betterment of schools and schooling in America.

Special Institutes or Programs

During the early 1950s, the Research Board (as it was called then) sponsored two Research Institutes to promote cooperative curriculum research. Later institutes involved scholars who made presentations about research in their various fields (e.g., anthropology, psychology, psychiatry) to ASCD member-participants as a way of upgrading the competence and understanding of practitioners in the field. Even later institutes involved participants in planning research activities that could be accomplished "back home" on topics that were of direct concern to ASCD members.

The number of ASCD members who participated in these special institutes and programs was always very small. However, because many of the programs resulted in publications that were distributed to the membership at large, the emphasis on research within ASCD has been pressed vigorously throughout the organization.

Publications

Like all major professional organizations that function at the national level, ASCD has always leaned heavily on publications as a way to bind the members together organizationally and thus provide a common thread of experience and information to which all members could relate.

Recognizing this reality of organizational life, the different committees that had responsibility for developing the research emphasis within ASCD sought permission from the Executive Council at various times to assume responsibility for preparing and disseminating, through publication, different documents that stressed the orientation of the committee.

Several different kinds of publications were produced over the years. For example, a special pamphlet series entitled, "What Does Research Say?" about various topics was produced. A column about research appeared regularly in *Educational Leadership* for a period of time. In 1957, the ASCD yearbook was devoted to research, the only such yearbook throughout the history of the organization. In chapter 4 of this book, William Alexander comments on the high quality of that yearbook, which was chaired by Arthur W. Foshay and James A. Hall.

In 1968, a special supplement to *Educational Leadership* reported research about curriculum and supervision. That supplement continued until 1974. Then, beginning in 1985, a new quarterly publication, the *Journal of Curriculum and Supervision*, was developed and funded by ASCD to report original research studies about curriculum.

The Role of ASCD in Research

ASCD has had a long-term involvement with and commitment to research in education. ASCD is not primarily a research organization, and never has been. Even so, the leaders and members of ASCD have consistently devoted time, money, energy, and thought to finding and creating ways that would encourage research, support research, report research, and use research to improve the quality of life for students, teachers, and others in the schools of America. That concern is still evident today.

8

ASCD and the Humanist Movement

ARTHUR W. COMBS
President, 1966-67

The enormous accomplishments of science and industry over the past three or four generations have confronted our society and a large portion of the Western world with a veritable revolution. For countless years humanity's greatest problems have been how to wrest from the environment the food, clothing, shelter, and security needed for ourselves and those we care for. Now science has given us the know-how and industry has developed the potential to feed, clothe, and house the entire world. At the same time, our technological successes have made possible enormous increases in population.

The net effect of all this has made us utterly dependent upon one another as never before in history. Today we live in the most cooperative, interdependent society the world has ever known, and every technological advance makes us more dependent than ever on the skills, cooperation, and good will of thousands of people we have never seen or heard of. The greatest problems humanity faces have shifted from things to people. Tick them off: the environment, pollution, civil rights, education, social security, family abuse, medical care, aging, war and peace, starvation, interdependent economies, women's lib, poverty, mental health—all human problems. Even the atomic bomb is a people problem. It is not the bomb we need fear but the folks who might use it!

While technological successes have created great new problems, they have also opened vast new possibilities for personal growth and development. For the first time in human history, millions of citizens are freed from the tyranny of preoccupation with survival and able to seek for need satisfaction in broader personal and social goals. One sees it in the search by millions of our citizens for greater personal fulfillment through education, health, exercise, nutrition, travel, sports, meditation, religion, and individual and group experiences of a hundred varieties.

This concern for human values, personal fulfillment, and effective human relationships is called the humanist movement. Its influence extends into every aspect of modern living. Today there are humanist movements in religion, medicine, civil rights, education, psychology, social work, anthropology, and political science. We have even invented a series of new professions to help us find solutions to human problems: clinical psychology, psychiatry, counseling, cultural anthropology, and pastoral counseling, for example. The major problem for everyone in the modern world is how to achieve more satisfying personal fulfillment as individuals and how to live effectively with others wherever they are encountered.

The Humanist Movement in Education

From its earliest days, ASCD has been deeply concerned about the human aspects of education. Many of the Association's charter members were strongly influenced by Dewey's philosophy and the progressive education movement of the late '30s and early '40s: They were attracted to the idea of learning as a deeply human, active function. Early national conferences placed heavy emphasis on group process, membership participation, and programs designed for maximum personal involvement in discussion groups, assemblies, workshops, and a variety of hands-on experiences. Consequently, the Association was ripe for the arrival of the humanist movement.

Of special import for education, the humanist movement focused attention on problems of the human condition being explored in the biological and social sciences. These explorations produced new insights about human need, growth, health, motivation, personality, and the importance of self-concept in human behavior. From biology came new and exciting understandings about the brain and its functioning. Perceptual-humanistic psychologists provided new concepts that shifted the focus of teaching and learning from acquisition of subject matter to the discovery of personal meaning and the facilitation of processes going on in the learner. In addition, the movement has the support of a broad scientific base in the concepts of modern sociology, anthropology, psychology, political science, and theology, as well as a rapidly expanding foundation of research corroboration previously unavailable.

These contributions were so significant for educators that the expression of the humanist movement in education has concentrated on three primary objectives:

1. Preparing youth to understand and cope with human interrelationships as individuals and in groups. This calls for the production of informed citizens, ready and willing to pull their own weight responsibly in an increasingly interdependent society.

2. Fostering the healthiest possible growth of students as individuals. This calls for educational programs designed to facilitate self-actualization and personal fulfillment.

3. Applying the very best understanding available from the biological and social sciences to forward the goals of education at every level.

The adoption of such goals in no way implies the abandonment of the traditional aims of education. Quite the contrary, the humanist movement in education only seeks to make the achievement of time-honored educational objectives more certain by recognizing the intensely human character of effective learning and using that knowledge to improve the processes of education.

The Influence of ASCD

With the end of "the last just war," the nation turned its attention to rebuilding its industrial and military potential. It was a time of ferment, change, and catching up. Times were good and millions of Americans sought to fulfill needs they had set aside during the war years. It was also a time of concern for human values and the rights of minorities, students, and women. Humanistic thinking found a warm reception in ASCD. The movement provided concepts and scientific support that many members already believed implicitly and experimented with in practice. In turn, the Association and its members gave further impetus to the movement through workshops, publications, national conferences, and the application of humanist thinking to educational problems and practice.

ASCD adopted a new organizational stance to "speak out" on social and political issues. ASCDers also reached out to incorporate many aspects of humanistic thinking being explored in psychology, sociology, anthropology, and political science. Humanistic leaders from these sciences were frequently asked to speak at national conferences, participate in workshops, or present their ideas in various ASCD publications. Many ASCD members became deeply involved in projects and innovations designed to implement humanistic thinking throughout educational practice from preschool to college and in supervision, administration, and curriculum reforms.

Perceiving, Behaving, Becoming

In 1962 ASCD published a yearbook entitled *Perceiving, Behaving, Becoming: A New Focus for Education*. Beginning with the assumption that a major objective of all education must be to contribute to the maximum health and fulfillment of its charges, the Yearbook Committee invited four humanistic psychologists and educators (Carl Rogers, Abraham Maslow, Earl Kelley, and myself) each to write a working paper on self-actualization, that is, to describe what a fully functioning, supremely healthy human being would be like. With these four papers in hand, the Yearbook Committee then asked, "If this is what supremely healthy human beings are like, what are the implications for educational theory and practice?" The answers they found appeared in the remainder of the yearbook. The response to this publication was phenomenal. The yearbook was an immediate success and continues so to the present. It has remained on the Association's best-seller list every year since its publication and has now sold over 100,000 copies. *Perceiving, Behaving, Becoming* also marked the beginning of a 20-year period of major interest in humanistic approaches to education's problems.

In 1965 the membership elected me, a humanistic psychologist and editor of the 1962 yearbook, as president of the Association. The year I took office, the theme of the annual conference was "Humanizing Education: The Person in the Process." The program featured such humanistic psychologists and educators as Carl Rogers, Earl Kelley, Sidney Jourard, William Van Til, Fred Wilhelms, and Donald Michael, to name a few.

The Contributions of ASCD

The relationship of ASCD and the humanist movement has continued ever since. Yearbooks between 1962 and 1980, for example, had such humanistically oriented titles as *Individualizing Instruction*; *Learning and Mental Health in the School*; *Youth Education: Problems, Perspectives, Promises*; *To Nurture Humaneness: Commitment for the '70s; A New Look At Progressive Education*; *Schools in*

Search of Meaning: Feeling, Valuing and the Art of Growing; and *Improving the Human Condition*. Other ASCD publications focused on such topics as *Dare to Care/Dare to Act: Racism and Education*; *Educational Accountability: Beyond Behavioral Objectives*; *Humanizing Education: The Person in The Process*; *Nurturing Individual Potential*; *Removing Barriers to Humaneness in The High School*; and *Humanistic Education: Objectives and Assessment*. Over the years, national conference programs and workshops reveal similar accents on humanist thought and action.

Opposition to Humanist Thought

The humanist movement in education has not been universally hailed. In the late '70s and early '80s, humanistic education was roundly denounced by some ultraconservatives of the "moral majority" and fundamentalist religious groups. They called the movement "secular humanism," claiming it was ungodly, communistically inspired, even a conspiracy to corrupt American youth. These tirades often fell on receptive ears, for public education was in a time of change and reassessment. In this climate, many people accepted the far right's shrill cries and held humanistic education responsible for many of the ills of public education. Some state and national legislatures even passed laws prohibiting the use of public funds for any program that smacked of the dreaded "secular humanism."

Much of the misunderstanding about the humanist movement in education arose from its name. Some people wrongly assumed that it was an arm of a philosophical school of thought that held that people ought not call on God to solve their problems but accept the responsibility for helping themselves. To many fundamentalist preachers that idea sounded like a sinful denial of the place of religion in life. Within the educational profession, many humanistically oriented teachers were bewildered and confused by all this as they found themselves labeled "ungodly," "soft," "harebrained," and worse, while their best efforts were decried as undemocratic, subversive, or antireligious.

Webster's New Twentieth Century Dictionary defines humanism as "1) the quality of being human; human nature, 2) any system or way of thought or action concerned with the interests and ideals of people." The *Oxford American Dictionary* defines a humanist as "a person who is concerned with the study of mankind and human affairs or who seeks to promote human welfare." What a paradox! A movement calling for greater understanding of youth, for the production of informed, responsible citizens, and for the application to learning of the best modern science has to offer was rejected and reviled by some as ungodly and un-American.

Despite the furor, the basic ideas of the humanist movement continue to flourish and find increasing expression in all aspects of American education. ASCD steadfastly maintains its long dedication to the "persons in the process" and continues to play a vital role in the humanistic movement. Its conferences, workshops, and publications provide important platforms for the dissemination and interpretation of humanistic ideas. Many ASCD members have made significant contributions to the movement through experimentation or by the introduction of humanistic principles to school curriculum, classroom practice, supervision, and administration, and a substantial number of ASCDers may be found among the leaders of the humanist movement in American education.

9

ASCD and Supervision: The Later Years

GERALD R. FIRTH
President, 1986-87

Across the years the search has continued to define the appropriate place of supervision in the activities of the Association for Supervision and Curriculum Development.

The Role of Supervision in ASCD

The tradition of ASCD—even its hallmark—of open membership has embraced different and often conflicting views of all professional and supportive roles in education. Nevertheless, those who represent public schools and higher education alike have long believed that stronger emphasis should be devoted to supervision as a field of study, to supervisors as a professional group, and to supervisory practice itself.

The Association has made many and substantive contributions to all three aspects of supervision. At many points during its development, ASCD was the only professional organization that provided attention to and leadership for instructional supervision. This chapter is intended to recognize the actors, actions, and accomplishments in supervision of which ASCD can be justly proud.

However, for all its convictions, any balanced analysis will show that ASCD has not yet realized its potential for supporting instructional supervision. Expression of belief has continued to ebb and flow with the result that periodically the concern is expressed to "put the 'S' back into ASCD."

The absence of a united front for instructional supervision is a result of the different conceptions held by sincere and vocal members of ASCD concerning the nature of supervision and those who provide it. Many maintain a traditional view that supervision is a function carried out by specific individuals in the central office of school districts; these individuals typically hold staff assignments under a vast array of titles and work directly with teachers in the improvement of classroom instruction. Many others in ASCD hold that supervision involves the broad range of leadership personnel who are engaged part or full time in numerous activities, including curriculum coordination and staff development.

In January 1970, Fred T. Wilhelms (executive secretary, 1968-71) emphasized the recurring concerns of supervision advocates with this statement:

For, in all truth, the Association has seldom devoted a major proportion of its energies directly to supervision. And it has put curiously little effort into applied curriculum development.[1]

At least one president, Muriel Crosby (president, 1968-69), strongly criticized ASCD for failure to assume in a number of ways its rightful role of leadership of supervisors and the field of supervision.

My personal conviction is that supervisors are the only staff members of many school systems whose energies are concentrated on helping teachers and improving learning; that supervisors have a wealth of potential for stimulating improvement in learning; and that they are being sold short by lack of effective leadership [within ASCD].[2]

Though boundaries and demarcation of eras are always arbitrary and often imprecise, it is appropriate here to consider the period between the publication of the 1965 yearbook and the 1982 yearbook as the later years of ASCD's involvement in supervision. The striking contrast in focus, content, and audience of the two publications perhaps describes the benchmarks of interest within and without the Association nearly two decades apart. The 1965 yearbook, *Role of The Supervisor and Curriculum Director in a Climate of Change*, devoted attention to professionalization of the supervisor among educational leaders, included information intended

---

[1] Association for Supervision and Curriculum Development, "A Report to the Membership," Fred T. Wilhelms, executive secretary, January 1970, p. 1.

[2] Muriel Crosby, "The New Supervisor: Caring, Coping, Becoming," in *Changing Supervision for Changing Times*, address before the 24th ASCD annual conference, Chicago, 16-20 March 1969, ed. Robert R. Leeper (Washington, D.C.: ASCD, 1969), p. 62.

to improve the status of supervisors, and served as a rallying cry for those committed to this goal.[3] The 1982 yearbook, *Supervision of Teaching*, provided broad perspective on the field of instructional supervision, examined various approaches as well as human factors and external forces.[4] The difference in content reflects an apparent change in the Association's conception of supervision from a function performed primarily by a small group of specialists to one performed by many leadership personnel, as well as by teachers themselves.

The zenith of interest in supervisors and supervision was reached in 1963 when the Commission on the Preparation of Instructional Leaders recommended that a requirement for ASCD membership be instituted by 1968, specifying two years of preparation beyond the baccalaureate degree from an approved institution of higher education for supervisors, curriculum workers, and professors of supervision and curriculum development.

In May 1964 the Committee on the Professionalization of Supervisors and Curriculum Workers, chaired by Gordon N. Mackenzie (president, 1955-56), urged such action by the Executive Committee and was invited to prepare a proposal for constitutional amendment defining appropriate membership qualifications.[5]

The report of the Steering Committee to the Board of Directors, considered at the October 1965 meeting of the Executive Committee, laid such a proposal to rest in the following manner:

The Steering Committee felt the suggestion of special membership requirements for ASCD would have the effect of changing the basic character of the Association and would disfranchise persons who now find a congenial home in the Association. Such an eventuality seemed to the Steering Committee a real tragedy to be avoided at any cost. The Committee is, however, deeply sympathetic to the dilemma of the supervisors in this matter. Accordingly, they suggested that the question of how the special needs of this group can be met under the general umbrella of ASCD remain an open and active question for the Board and future Steering Committees.[6]

Other proposals of the Committee on Professionalization of Supervisors and Curriculum Workers—particularly relating to theory development, certification, and accreditation of preparation pro-

[3] Robert R. Leeper, ed., *Role of the Supervisor and Curriculum Director in a Climate of Change*, 1965 ASCD yearbook (Washington, D.C.: ASCD, 1965).

[4] Thomas J. Sergiovanni, ed., *Supervision of Teaching*, 1982 ASCD yearbook (Alexandria, Va.: ASCD, 1982).

[5] Minutes of the Meeting of ASCD Executive Committee, May 1964.

[6] Minutes of the Meeting of ASCD Executive Committee, October 1965.

grams—have received attention from the Association in ways that are discussed later.

Throughout its history, many individuals and groups within ASCD have demonstrated support for supervision. Often that support has come from unexpected sources. Psychologist Arthur W. Combs (President, 1966-67) proposed a professional board for supervisors. Intended to create a professional home for supervisors, Combs' proposal embraced issues of preparation, certification, and conduct of supervisors. The Board of Directors rejected the plan. Despite their agreement on the problems faced by supervisors, the majority felt that any action singling out a particular group was inherently divisive and potentially disintegrative to an organization with diverse membership.[7]

In March 1967, during his inaugural address as incoming ASCD president, J. Harlan Shores declared that he would make the Association "a home for supervisors." Whatever his aspirations for increasing the organization's focus on supervision, Shores' plan was unsuccessful. A year later in Chicago, a major confrontation with the counterculture caused a reduction of energies and a searching of conscience by the Association that dramatically influenced its structure, policies, programs, and, perhaps, destiny.

Ten years of increased attention to supervision and expanded interest in that area were thwarted by that confrontation. It disrupted the only annual conference devoted to supervision and resulted in the resignation of then president Muriel Crosby, one of the strongest allies of supervision.

Ironically, one of the few general session speeches dealing directly with supervision was never delivered because of Crosby's early departure. Later published with other addresses in *Changing Supervision for Changing Times*, her call for "The New Supervisor: Caring, Coping, Becoming" echoed a continuing concern that supervisors are weary of being sent without assistance to change the world and included a plea to equip them to be more effective:

Supervisors cry in all earnestness. "We don't need to be told that the world is changing. We need to be helped to create new understandings, new strategies in helping teachers cope with change. More than this, we need help in creating with others a new education for this new world."[8]

The 1969 annual conference in Chicago has been regarded as a watershed for ASCD. The Wilhelms Report in January 1970 summarizes part of the organizational effects:

---

[7] Minutes of the Meeting of the ASCD Board of Directors, March 1967.
[8] Muriel Crosby, ibid., p. 46.

Chicago: that turbulent, emotional week; dismaying to some, challenging, even exhilarating, to others. Whatever the rights of that may have been, the conference epitomized much that was to characterize the year: a deepening concern for all minority groups not well served by the schools, outreach for a broader, more diverse membership base, drive for expanded and harder-hitting programs of action.[9]

Aside from the emotional trauma sustained by its members and the fiscal havoc wrought on the organization during the Chicago conference and its aftermath, many lament the permanent derailment of the movement to upgrade and professionalize the roles of instructional supervisors and curriculum leaders. The high water mark had been reached—and lost—within a few hours.

Never again has there been the ambitious and intensive support for supervision advocated by Crosby. Although reflected in its publications, programs, and projects, supervision has never regained that position of prominence within ASCD, a circumstance all the more surprising in view of the accelerating number and proportion of membership drawn from leadership in public schools.

ASCD-Sponsored Activities

ASCD-sponsored activities related to supervision consist of its councils, commissions, committees, and working groups; publications and resource materials; annual conferences; and national curriculum study institutes or research institutes.

Councils, Commissions, Committees, and Working Groups

At the 1959 annual conference, the Association adopted a resolution that created a Commission on the Preparation of Instructional Leaders.[10] Much of the credit for the success of the group and the movement that it set in motion is attributed to the dedication and perception of its first chair, Gordon N. Mackenzie (president, 1955-56). Upon recommendation of this commission, the Executive Committee in 1961 committed ASCD to cooperating with the American Association of School Administrators, the Department of Elementary School Principals, and the National Association of Secondary School Principals in establishing a Joint Committee on the

---

[9] Association for Supervision and Curriculum Development, "A Report to the Membership," Fred T. Wilhelms, executive secretary, January 1970, p. 5.

[10] James R. Ogletree, "Professionalization of Supervisors and Curriculum Workers," *Educational Leadership* 23 (November 1965): 153.

Professionalization of Administrators and Supervisors.[11]

At this point, two significant committees were appointed that individually and in combination were to exert considerable influence on Association policies, programs, and projects.

According to the minutes of the Executive Committee, the Commission on Supervision Theory was appointed in October 1962. A simultaneous motion made by William Van Til (president, 1961-62) and seconded by Alexander Frazier (president, 1969-70) authorized the Executive Committee to initiate simultaneously two new commissions: one on Curriculum Theory and another on Supervision Theory.[12] Kimball Wiles, in his capacity as ASCD president, charged the latter group:

To take leadership in the formulation of a theory of supervision based on an analysis of the research in leadership, communication, community power structure, decision making, the process of change and other relevant areas. It is hoped that the Commission will accept the responsibility for planning and conducting seminars or institutes or other appropriate activities centered around an exploration of segments of research statements and interpretations that are important in evolving a theory of supervision.[13]

John T. Lovell was appointed to chair the ten-member Commission on Supervision Theory in 1963. Unable to agree on a unified position statement or plan for action after several meetings, its members published the results of extensive deliberations in the 1967 report, *Supervision: Perspectives and Propositions*. Lovell's chapter, "A Perspective for Viewing Instructional Supervisory Behavior," advanced a systems approach to instructional supervision.[14]

At its meeting in May 1963, the Executive Committee accepted the report from the Commission on the Preparation of Instructional Leaders and changed the group's name to the Committee on Professionalization of Supervisors and Curriculum Workers.[15] The committee was given the charge to explore six areas: role clarification, selection, preparation, accreditation, certification, and membership responsibilities. James R. (Bob) Ogletree initially chaired this

[11] Ibid., p. 154.
[12] Minutes of the Meeting of the ASCD Executive Committee, October 1962.
[13] Ibid.
[14] John T. Lovell, "A Perspective for Viewing Instructional Supervisory Behavior," in *Supervision: Perspectives and Propositions* (Washington, D.C.: ASCD, 1967), pp. 12-28.
[15] Minutes of the Meeting of the ASCD Executive Committee, May 1963.

committee; Harold T. Shafer succeeded him in 1966. The committee developed a working paper on "The Role of the Curriculum Supervisor," which was discussed at the 1964 annual conference.[16]

Much of the material drawn from working papers of the Committee on Professionalization of Supervisors and Curriculum Workers was published in the 1967 booklet, *Toward Professional Maturity of Supervisors and Curriculum Workers*, for which Shafer served as editor.[17]

Perhaps the highlight of the efforts by the Commission on Professionalization of Supervisors and Curriculum Workers was the three-day symposium on "The Supervisor: New Demands, New Dimensions," sponsored at New Orleans in December 1967. The major papers of the symposium, edited by William H. Lucio, were published under the same title in 1969.[18]

In 1968 a single Commission on Problems of Supervisors and Curriculum Workers, chaired by Shafer, was formed to carry through the concerns of the former Committee on the Professionalization of Supervisors and Curriculum workers and the work of the Commission on Supervision Theory.[19] A project undertaken by a subcommittee of the Commission on Problems of Supervisors and Curriculum Workers resulted in a report on research from leadership, communications, organizations, and change. When a series of circumstances beginning with a strike of local unions in San Francisco just preceding and during the 1970 annual conference produced financial reversals for the Association, the report was released for publication in the private sector. Material from this report became a central piece of one textbook[20] and provided key elements of another.[21]

A Supervision Council with Robert Harnack as chair and a Commission on Negotiations and Supervisory Staff Relationship with William F. Young as chair were appointed by the Executive

---

[16] Minutes of the Meeting of the ASCD Executive Committee, April 1965.

[17] Harold T. Shafer, ed., *Toward Professional Maturity of Supervisors and Curriculum Workers* (Washington, D.C.: ASCD, 1967).

[18] William H. Lucio, ed., *The Supervisor: New Demands, New Dimensions* (Washington, D.C.: ASCD, 1969).

[19] Association for Supervision and Curriculum Development, *Annual Report* (Washington, D.C.: ASCD, 1968), p. 12.

[20] Robert J. Alfonso, Gerald R. Firth, and Richard F. Neville, *Instructional Supervision: A Behavior System* (Boston: Allyn and Bacon, 1975).

[21] Kimball Wiles and John T. Lovell, *Supervision for Better Schools*, 4th ed. (Englewood Cliffs, N.J.: Prentice-Hall, 1975).

Council in 1969.[22] A publication developed by a subcommittee under Bernard W. Kinsella described the dilemma of instructional supervisors and/or curriculum leaders regarding attempts to clarify their functions in collective bargaining.[23]

A Working Group on Supervisory Practices appointed in 1975 and chaired by Robert J. Alfonso conducted a national survey.[24] Its 1976 report on "Issues in Supervisor Roles: What Do Practitioners Say?" indicated that supervisory practice had not changed appreciably in the previous five years.[25]

In 1976 a Working Group on Accreditation and Certification of Curriculum Leaders and Supervisors, chaired by Allan W. Sturges, was charged by the Executive Council with developing guidelines for the approval of preparation programs and certification to practice.[26] Using the designation of Role, Function, and Preparation of the Curriculum Worker, this group prepared a publication on *Curriculum Leaders: Improving Their Influence*[27] in 1976, the *Standards and Guidelines for Evaluation of Graduate Programs Preparing Curriculum Leaders*[28] in 1977, and a companion statement, *Certificating the Curriculum Leader and the Instructional Supervisor*[29] in 1978. Another group was established by the Executive Council in October 1977 through funding a proposal from Sturges on the Roles and Responsibilities of Supervisors.[30]

ASCD then embarked on a series of short-term activities in the field, consisting in 1979 and 1980 of a Commission on Organizing Schools for Supervision/Instructional Improvement chaired by

[22] Minutes of the Meeting of the ASCD Executive Council, May 1969.

[23] William F. Young, ed., *The Supervisor's Role in Negotiation* (Washington, D.C.: ASCD, 1969).

[24] Minutes of the Meeting of the ASCD Executive Council, October 1975.

[25] ASCD Working Group on Supervisor Practices, "Issues in Supervisor Roles: What Do Practitioners Say?" *Educational Leadership* 34 (December 1976): 217-220.

[26] Minutes of the Meeting of the ASCD Executive Council, June 1976.

[27] Charles A. Speiker, ed., *Curriculum Leaders: Improving Their Influence* (Washington, D.C.: ASCD, 1976).

[28] Association for Supervision and Curriculum Development, *Standards and Guidelines for Evaluation of Graduate Programs Preparing Curriculum Leaders* (Alexandria, Va.: ASCD, [1977] 1983).

[29] Allan W. Sturges, ed., *Certificating the Curriculum Leader and the Instructional Supervisor,* a report of the ASCD Working Group on the Role, Preparation, and Certification of Curriculum Leaders and Supervisors (Alexandria, Va.: ASCD, 1978).

[30] Minutes of the Meeting of the ASCD Executive Council, October 1977.

Charles Reavis,[31] in 1981 of a study on Comparison of the Effectiveness of Supervision Practice chaired by Donald Fett,[32] and in 1982 and 1983 of a Working Group on Effective Approaches to Supervision chaired by Robert Anderson.[33] A project on Supervision and Leader Behavior Training was chaired in 1984 by Ben Harris and in 1985 by Dale Mann.[34]

A Commission on Instructional Supervision composed of 78 individuals from public school districts, institutions of higher education, and professional agencies was appointed by the Executive Council for a two year period in 1984.[35] George Goens chaired that group.

Publications

Of the 2,677 articles that appeared in the 200 issues of *Educational Leadership* published from 1960-61 through 1984-85, 328 articles or 12 percent were devoted to instructional supervision. Only four times (1962-63, 1963-64, 1965-66, and 1976-77) did the proportion approach a quarter of the articles published in a particular year. For 10 of the 25 years involved, articles on instructional supervision made up less than 10 percent of those published each year.

On nine occasions, "Instructional Supervision" constituted the theme of an issue. "Staff Development" was highlighted in four issues. The broader topic of "Leadership" has received more emphasis, serving as the theme on 12 occasions.

Between 1961 and 1984, ASCD published 13 booklets, prepared seven audiotapes, and developed four videotapes on supervision. Approximately half of the supervision-related booklets appearing between 1960 and 1985 were devoted to the professionalization of the supervisor; the remainder focused on selected aspects of supervisory practice, mirroring the themes of the 1965 and 1982 yearbooks.

From 1960 to 1985, ASCD released three booklets, one audio-

---

[31] Minutes of the Meeting of the ASCD Executive Council, October 1978.

[32] Minutes of the Meeting of the ASCD Executive Council, October 1980.

[33] Minutes of the Meeting of the ASCD Executive Council, October 1982.

[34] Minutes of the Meeting of the ASCD Executive Council, October 1983.

[35] Minutes of the Meeting of the ASCD Executive Council, October 1984.

tape, and one videotape on staff development. During the same period, ASCD developed one booklet, ten audiotapes, and two videotapes on the topic of leadership. Another 16 booklets that contain some attention to supervision were produced during that same period.

Several articles on the theme of professionalization of supervisors were published in various issues of *Educational Leadership* and subsequently were aggregated into a 1969 publication entitled *Supervision: Emerging Profession*.[36] Another collection, *Readings in Educational Supervision*, compiled from *Educational Leadership* by Edith E. Grimsley and Ray E. Bruce in 1982, also has become popular as a supplementary text.[37]

Premiering in the fall of 1985, the *Journal of Curriculum and Supervision* provides a research focus on the two fields reflected in its title.

Annual Conference

Only the 1969 annual conference in Chicago on "Changing Supervision for Changing Times" gave focus to a theme directly related to supervision. Perhaps its closest approximation in the quarter century from 1960 through 1985 occurred at Anaheim in 1982 with the theme "Leadership in Education for a New Century."

Another index to ASCD's concern for supervision is the number of related sessions conducted as part of the program of the annual conferences, typically 2 to 7 percent of the total number. The highest number of sessions devoted to supervision occurred at conferences in Chicago (1969), Atlanta (1980), St. Louis (1981), and Anaheim (1982). The latter program contained a record 69 percent of 173 sessions devoted to supervisory topics, issues, and concerns.

National Curriculum Study Institutes

Perhaps the most visible indicator of attention by ASCD is the number of National Curriculum Study Institutes devoted to supervisory practice. Of the first 11 NCSI sessions conducted in 1974-75, only one focused on supervision. In 1984-85 when the number of NCSI sessions had reached 61, nine focused on supervision.

Of the 290 NCSIs conducted from 1974 through 1985, the number of those directly focused on supervision was only 35, a modest

---

[36] Robert L. Leeper, ed., *Supervision: Emerging Profession* (Washington, D.C.: ASCD, 1969).

[37] Edith E. Grimsley and Ray E. Bruce, eds., *Readings in Educational Supervision* (Alexandria, Va.: ASCD, 1982).

12 percent. However, inclusion of those involving staff development and leadership increases the proportion to 25 percent. The NCSI series projected for 1985-86 focuses on supervision at the median rate.

In contrast, supervision-related themes were conspicuous by their absence from ASCD Research Institutes, which preceded the NCSI program. Of the 25 Research Institutes conducted between 1955 and 1969 (usually two per year) only two focused on supervision.

ASCD-Promoted Activities in Related Organizations

The matter of accreditation of preparation programs for instructional supervisors and curriculum directors dates from early deliberations of the Commission on the Preparation of Instructional Leaders. That Commission's report to the ASCD Executive Committee in May 1963 recommended the designation of the National Council for Accreditation of Teacher Education (NCATE) as the appropriate agency to approve graduate programs in supervision and curriculum.[38]

The impetus of this early commitment led eventually to the generation of respective guidelines accepted by NCATE for approval of preparation of instructional supervisors and of curriculum leaders. For several years ASCD committees worked cooperatively with NCATE "in planning for accreditation and in supporting the accreditation process."[39]

The *Standards and Guidelines for Evaluation of Graduate Programs Preparing Curriculum Leaders*, published originally by ASCD in 1977-78 and revised in 1982-83, evolved through several stages of development due to the dedicated efforts of the Working Group on Accreditation and Certification of Curriculum Leaders and Supervisors.[40] A working copy of the standards was developed originally from data collected for the 1976 publication on *Curriculum Leaders: Improving Their Influence*.[41]

Unfortunately, the prospects of ASCD involvement in the accre-

---

[38] Minutes of the Meeting of the ASCD Executive Committee, May 1963.

[39] Harold T. Shafer and Gordon N. Mackenzie, "Securing Competent Instructional Leaders," in *Role of the Supervisor and Curriculum Director in a Climate of Change*, 1965 ASCD yearbook, ed. Robert R. Leeper (Washington, D.C.: ASCD, 1969), p. 83.

[40] *Standards and Guidelines*, ibid.

[41] Charles A. Speiker, ibid.

ditation process were never fully implemented, although volunteers for membership on visiting teams attended the orientation workshops at several annual conferences. Much the same result occurred in regard to implementation of the proposed requirements for certification of instructional supervisors and curriculum leaders. However, experience indicates that greater progress was achieved when the state affiliates of ASCD took the cause directly to their respective state departments of education. Due to complexities in organizational structure, it is impossible to determine which recommendations for changes in certification have been stimulated by ASCD affiliates and which by individuals holding ASCD membership but working through other state organizations.

Activities Generated in Other Organizations

A group of ASCD members concerned about the "loss of the 'S' in ASCD" began in the early 1970s to seek a method to foster their interest through a separate but related organization. Emulating the Professors of Curriculum, which had met during the annual conference of ASCD for some years, a small group met in 1975 in New Orleans. They planned the Council of Professors of Instructional Supervision (COPIS) and established the group officially the following year during the ASCD annual conference in Miami. Fourteen individuals accepted invitations to attend the organizational meeting to become charter members of COPIS. In 1978, the first Invitational Conference of COPIS was held at Kent State University, initiating a pattern of a separate meeting each year, hosted by an institution of higher learning, in addition to the meeting at the ASCD annual conference.

More recently, COPIS members also active within the American Educational Research Association formed a Special Interest Group (SIG) on Instructional Supervision. In August 1983, Instructional Supervision officially became the 32nd active AERA/SIG and conducted its first program sessions at the April 1983 meeting of AERA in Montreal. The SIG started with 30 members and has quickly grown to over 100 members. The congruence among faculty at institutions of higher education listed as members of COPIS, AERA/SIG, and ASCD is extraordinary.

The Need for Attention to Supervision

The continuing concern raised by advocates of supervision is more of degree than kind. Certainly ASCD has devoted some attention to supervision throughout its 43-year history. However, emphases on the field, its role, and its practitioners have been, at best, uneven and, at worst, disjointed. The significance—or lack of significance—of supervision and supervisors to ASCD in recent years is reflected in a low percentage of supervisor members and supervision activities—programs, publications, and projects.

Perhaps the call for action now as then is expressed in the preface to the 1977 report of the ASCD Working Group on the Role, Preparation, and Certification of Curriculum Leaders and Supervisors:

Unless the membership of ASCD is immediately responsive, the opportunity to influence decision . . . may diminish or disappear. Even now, the political climate makes our actions difficult. Nothing less than the marshalling of unified professional statemanship can ensure that those who bear the titles of curriculum directors and instructional supervisors possess those unique characteristics and skills which are essential for serving effectively in their named roles the educational enterprise in these times.[42]

Supervision will receive emphasis during my presidency of ASCD, 1986-1987. Leadership and supervision will be addressed in varied Association activities from 1986 throughout 1989, for effective leadership and supervisory behavior has been designated as one of the major areas of focus of the Five-Year Plan adopted in 1985 by the Executive Council.

---

[42] Gerald R. Firth, "Preface," in *Certificating the Curriculum Leader and Instructional Supervisor*, ed., Allan W. Sturges (Alexandria, Va.: ASCD, 1978), p. ii.

10

ASCD and Curriculum Development: The Later Years

O. L. DAVIS, JR.
President, 1982-83

Curriculum development has been a prominent concern of the Association for Supervision and Curriculum Development during the past 20 years. However, to some, members and nonmembers alike, ASCD's concern has not involved real attention to curriculum development at all, but instead has focused vigorously on instruction and management under the symbolic banner of curriculum development. To others, ASCD's program and governance policy decisions have ignored supervision and, particularly, school supervisors. They allege that this displacement of these historical and equal ASCD functions has disproportionately favored curriculum development. Others insist that ASCD's concern for curriculum development continues as a lively element in the Association, albeit one filled with tension.

Roots of these perceptions and disputations sink deeply into the soil of the Association's early years. Differing views on ASCD's role in curriculum development have been expressed during the social and educational ferment of the later years.

A major factor influencing these positions in the past two decades must be acknowledged. The Association, accustomed to a largely stable and rather low membership (and income) during its first 20 years, has seen its membership skyrocket from some 12,000 13 years ago to 70,000 today. Clearly, ASCD is not the organization

now that it was 20 years ago. Change in the organization has accompanied altered perceptions, changed meanings, and different
activities.

Thus, any understanding of ASCD and curriculum development
must penetrate language and practice, policy and perceptions, as
well as programs and governance. This chapter is an exploration of
these features of the ASCD experience during the second half of the
Association's history. Only a few specific examples can be chosen to
illuminate this exploration.

The Role of a Professional Organization

Views of professional organizations and their effect on professional practice must be constrained by understandings of their
roles. What a voluntary association of individuals may engage in
and accomplish understandably has limits. ASCD, like most voluntary professional associations, has attracted members who possess individual affinity with organizational purposes and programs. Thus, membership in ASCD, certainly for continuing
members, has attested to the individual's interests in the functions
of curriculum development and supervision, mainly in local school
settings. Because of such interests, members have purchased services and products that have included publications and conferences
and have received opportunities for continuing education in curriculum development and supervision.

ASCD has not developed school curriculums. Neither its purpose nor its resources have been or are appropriate to such a task.
Indeed, the term "for curriculum development" in the Association's
name explicitly asserts the historical intention of ASCD to foster,
advance, and improve curriculum development as practiced. To
honor this intent, ASCD welcomed to membership all interested in
its purpose, not just individuals with assigned roles in curriculum
development and supervision.

Imbedded in this historical background was agreement by
ASCD members on the integral relationship of curriculum, instruction, and supervision in concept and in practice. This understanding flowered from the extensive school-based curriculum efforts of
the 1920s and 1930s and entered the new ASCD as shared language
and meanings. The role of the Association, consistent with such
shared understandings, was implemented by publications, conferences, and an expanding governance outreach to state and regional
affiliates. This role was one of education on behalf of ASCD's shared
understandings, through a variety of forums for discussion, analy-

sis, and reflection.

The historic role of ASCD has been tested and reconceptualized during the past 20 years. For example, during the era of discipline-centered curriculum reforms, some in ASCD believed the organization had been bypassed and school curriculum specialists disregarded, so they called for greater involvement by ASCD in developing reform proposals. Others believed that ASCD's role should be that of a gatekeeper to the schools to admit or to refuse admission of newly developed curriculums. Both positions claimed more territory and power than a voluntary professional organization can possess in this society, and both were disappointed. However, during this era, ASCD did make impressive contributions to leaders in local schools and their work in adoption, revision, and use of these curriculums. Conference programs and publications featured the national project materials through exposition, analysis, demonstration, and exhibit; debates and data presentations critiqued project claims. ASCD provided its members and the profession at large with deliberation and discussion and contributed therewith to the enhanced possibility of curriculum development in local schools.

Use of computers in schools represents a similar case in recent years. Again, ASCD's role as forum has brought information and respected commentary to the attention of school leaders. However, ASCD has not endorsed specific computer systems or software; neither has it produced/developed software for use in school programs.

These instances illuminate the actual role of ASCD today in curriculum development. ASCD as a body does not cause things to happen in school programs and in instruction by promoting specific curriculums. Rather, through its role as forum, it serves individuals, members in the main, who are instrumental in curriculum decisions in local schools.

Language and Practice

As observed earlier, the function of curriculum development emerged from the practice of curriculum improvement efforts in local schools during the 1920s and '30s. The term "curriculum development" gradually replaced "curriculum construction" because the latter simply could not withstand the results of its failed practice. Curriculum development includes the completed artifacts of curriculum (e.g., courses of study, units, lessons) and the process of local curriculum inquiry (e.g., study, planning), decision making (by those affected by the decisions), and development of the ideas and skills integral to the focus of the curriculum development effort.

In practice, curriculum development interrelates with supervision and relates intimately to processes associated with the improvement of classroom instruction.

The curriculum development function as described previously was maintained and elaborated in ASCD during the first 15 to 20 years of its existence. The annual ASCD conference was established and continued as an event to which participants would come to study, to deliberate and discuss, to observe school practice, and, in the conference format, to practice and self-consciously reflect upon both individual and group knowledge and skills important to group leadership and group maintenance and productivity. In this context of shared meaning, the concept and practice of action research took root and was nourished. Shared inquiry on real problems characterized both substance and process; it was illuminated in conferences and publications as well as practiced in Association governance.

As years passed, everyday usage in education slowly corrupted "curriculum development" into a shortened term, "curriculum." This term was invested with renewed meanings, which served to alter that to which it referred in practice while elevating its symbolic potency. "Curriculum" came to be used in mostly nonrestricted ways to denote curriculum, instruction, teaching, and even education, all laced together in the one word. "Curriculum" may well be seen as dominating both ASCD and schooling's practice and discourse. This change in meanings and usage was not suddenly achieved. Probably, it is the companion of sociological and philosophic alterations in the mind-scape of the larger education profession. Unquestionably, however, this change overtook ASCD through its members and their everyday professional practice and talk about their work.

Thus, those whose major professional interest is the supervision of instruction find themselves in a sea of discourse about curriculum even when the subjects of the sentences are supervisors and supervision. Many have become weary of this language overload and have petitioned for separate, distinguishable Association elements centering on supervision. Those whose professional concern is the curriculum and curriculum development as historically understood have alleged that the organization has abandoned them and their interests by substituting a focus on instruction and management in the Association's program. These conceptual and political problems are real. Yet they have been dismissed too frequently in recent years as special pleading.

Concerned ASCD members have addressed stubborn language

problems in our field, such as varied interpretations of the term curriculum. Notably, Dwayne Huebner and James Macdonald early fostered the analyses of meanings. Their conference addresses, articles, and yearbook chapters have attracted attention and stimulated awareness of many in the field to the exploration of meanings in professional language.

ASCD, like other voluntary professional organizations, can maintain no authorized meanings. Thus, the Association's policies and programs reflect the "growth" of meanings about curriculum and curriculum development. For instance, now even the annual ASCD conference is styled as "the most comprehensive *instructional* conference in America" (emphasis added). The conference program no longer emphasizes study and discussion; for the most part, it showcases assertedly new school programs, practices, and techniques mostly through single sessions and provides audiences for the advocacy of ideas and programs.

The success of ASCD in attracting members is beyond dispute. The Association's symbols and program elements obviously strike a responsive, positive chord within the profession. For example, recent annual conferences are popular and, quite obviously, fulfill the expectations and needs of current members in attendance.

The contemporary meanings of curriculum and curriculum development clearly have power. That they differ from the meanings in widespread use a quarter-century ago merits acknowledgment and understanding as ASCD experiences steady change and growth. Curriculum development remains a viable ASCD concern. The term and practices associated with it have changed profoundly over recent years.

Constituency and Affiliation

Throughout its first 20 years, ASCD's asserted constituency, its potential membership, included everyone interested in curriculum development and the improvement of instruction. Constitutionally inclusive of all "involved in the process," membership in actuality was made up mainly of two groups of curriculum and supervision specialists. One group consisted principally of central office curriculum workers and supervisors. Some senior system and building administrators and a few teachers were also a part of this group. The other group, much smaller in number, consisted mostly of college professors of curriculum and instruction. The career history of individuals in this latter group commonly included curriculum development and supervisory experience in schools. Since each group largely shared a common concern for the Association's foci and understandings and also shared similar occupational backgrounds, only rarely were these groupings of roles identified with internal ASCD political issues or differences of opinion. By the late 1960s, however, the historical constituency began to dissolve.

The context for this development was expansion—the rapid expansion of school services occasioned by the availability of federal funding (through the NDEA and ESEA, specifically) and the robust expansion of higher education during the same years. Simply put, ASCD's original general constituency was diminished. Yet ASCD membership expanded in a very short time. The earlier sense of affiliation was reconstructed into new forms.

The Association's long-standing desire to increase membership rapidly became a realizable prospect with the addition of new district central office personnel funded by newly available federal resources. Many of these individuals had recently been building and system administrators. Coincidentally, the Association's efforts to expand and strengthen state and regional affiliates began to pay handsome dividends. Membership in many affiliates grew quickly. A significant part of the growth represented newcomers to central office staffs and their associates, building and system administrators. These newcomers to ASCD and its program sought professional insights and credibility and desired them rapidly. Their interest in actively participating in Association affairs promptly swept a number into leadership positions, a trend that persists.

Involvement of large city curriculum leaders in ASCD was a special deliberate effort during the late 1960s and through the 1970s. These individuals from the nation's major metropolitan centers were recognized as missing from conferences and other ASCD activities. They were not hostile to ASCD; they were not participating for several reasons. Foremost among them were (a) their engagement in complex, often intense confrontations at home and the overwhelming magnitude of problems attendant to schooling in urban centers, and (b) their perception that ASCD's program had little of value to assist them in their professional endeavors. A major ASCD initiative was the Urban Curriculum Leaders Conference, an initial meeting of large city curriculum leaders. This conference was well received immediately, has prospered over the years, and has stimulated increased involvement of the urban leaders in ASCD programs and governance.

Another impressive move, launched in the early 1970s, was the deliberate marketing of memberships by means of direct mail. These campaigns reaped immediately successful results and were transformed into a regular feature of the Association's membership promotion. Though not without early vigorous opposition, direct mail promotion must be credited for most of the spectacular rise in membership during the last decade.

Because of these and other promotional affairs, composition of the Association's membership has been altered fundamentally. Building principals currently comprise the largest membership category, followed closely by other administrators. College professors, never a large group within the Association, now constitute a very small segment of the membership.

The change in Association membership has prompted some ASCD program shifts and legitimated others. Training, for example, has assumed a prominent role through the ASCD National Curriculum Study Institutes. Very popular, these institutes are conceived as instructional settings for information and skills related to matters perceived as important and, as well, topical. Staffed by highly visible authorities, they meet busy administrators' needs to secure desired knowledge and skills quickly and efficiently. Major revision of *Educational Leadership;* a second illustration, has characterized its transition into a bright journalistic magazine designed to be read by busy administrators. While continuing to address substantial and complex matters, most articles in an issue showcase practices and policies in schools. Only a few articles critically examine issues or probe to reveal meanings in proposals and current practice; even fewer report research evidence. Yet the Association's official journal does regularly publish some major conceptual papers. *Educational Leadership* steadily garners prizes in the education press and praise from ASCD members and other readers. Quite simply, such ASCD program activities reflect the profound change in the ASCD constituency.

The other significant shift in ASCD's historical constituency was occasioned during the expansion of higher education during the 1960s and 1970s. Many entrants into university curriculum studies faculties were unlike their predecessors. Since they entered into university teaching early in their careers, their professional experience was more limited; fewer shared the building and system leadership experience in curriculum development that has characterized many who preceded them. Many of these newcomers participated in ASCD activities, but another set of forces constrained their active involvement in the Association.

One of these forces was within ASCD. It took various forms but was characterized by a growing sense that the steadily expanding Association valued practitioners and immediate practice more than it did nonpractitioners (i.e., college professors) and reflections about practice. This unfortunate dichotomy of thought politically separated practitioners and professors. Since the practitioner majority continued to increase, college professors became progressively isolated, in perception and reality, particularly in many affiliates and, later, in Association governance.

Another force was the social dynamics and reward structure in higher education. Research, publication, and peer review were standards by which a professional career might be shattered or brightened. ASCD has never been known as an organization for researchers. Additionally, the scholarly demands of peer (juried) review of manuscripts chosen for publication and of papers for presentation at conferences were irrelevant to the Association's history and its policies. University-based ASCD members, thus, found themselves caught in an especially virulent double bind. Not only were they and their participation isolated (or so many of them believed), their ASCD activities and publications, if any, were not highly valued by their university tenure and promotion committees.

Consequently, during the 1960s university professors of curriculum studies began a shift of organization focus from ASCD to other groups, particularly to Division B of the American Educational Research Association. There, their role as professors was not devalued since AERA provided a showcase of juried papers at the annual convention and forums for the lively discussion and intense debate of issues and topics unconstrained by the necessity to relate ideas to immediate practice. In university reward systems, AERA participation became more valued than involvement in ASCD and similar groups.

Attendant to this change was the practical necessity of professors to choose one national meeting to attend. The 1970s, in particular, saw rapid increases in costs of conference transportation and housing. Professors might be reimbursed in part by their institution for one trip each year, but seldom for more than one trip. As costs rose, a number of professors who were active in both ASCD and AERA were forced by personal economics to choose one conference to attend. Many professors, particularly the younger ones, not surprisingly cast their lot with AERA.

So ASCD's constituency changed dramatically throughout the 1970s and '80s. This change altered the Association's intellectual contributions to curriculum development, long recognized as very strong. It deprived both practice and reflection on practice of the mutual nourishment they had enjoyed since ASCD's birth.

A desired rapprochment has been the subject of several recent deliberate efforts within the Association. Most dramatic has been the establishment of a new quarterly ASCD journal, the *Journal of Curriculum and Supervision*, which publishes juried research reports and scholarly analyses and critiques. Considered off and on for almost 27 years, the decision to launch this new journal communicates as official ASCD policy an intention to give serious attention both to scholarship (even theory) and to some of the interests of its university faculty members. Another new initiative is the encouragement of networks of ASCD members. One of these networks links a number of ASCDers who are university professors. These efforts appear to be important, albeit modest and hesitant; others need to be invented and quickly implemented.

Publications and Programs

Educational Leadership continues as ASCD's most visible service to members and the profession. The journal, earlier noted to have shifted in format and focus in the past 20 years, persistently offers through its pages descriptions and informed commentary on matters significant to current curriculum and instruction leadership. Surveys throughout the period reveal a balanced treatment of topics. Most practicing curriculum leaders attest that they would not be as informed as they are without this major Association journal.

Not only *Educational Leadership* has changed during these past 20 years. Slowly and self-consciously until very recently, the Association's publications efforts are being reconceptualized. Some elements of this program continue to be offered as direct membership services—*Educational Leadership*, the yearbook, and four smaller books. Other elements, specifically some books, audiotapes, videotapes, and an expanding journal program (including the *Journal of Curriculum and Supervision*) are offered as important products of the Association to special segments of the membership and the profession at large. This second group of products has enjoyed massive growth during the past decade and has become a major profit center for the Association. ASCD has created new in-house publishing and marketing operations that serve the Association membership both directly and indirectly.

Increased in-house editorial management, from idea generation through selection of writers and producers, oversight of manuscript preparation, and timely production controls, are consequences of these larger changes. Editorial personnel now have a more active role in policy formulation. Publications in book form continue to be recognized as valued resources in the ASCD publication program. Now, however, videotapes are also seen as major substantive Association products. The publications group continues to monitor other technologies and to consider revised and new publication offerings. Most recently, an audiotape version of *Educational Leadership* has been marketed. Videodiscs and computer networking are among elements of publications that may soon be available.

The number of working groups within the Association has decreased. Earlier known as committees and commissions, these groups seldom received sufficient funding. Nevertheless, most of them, including many in the curriculum development area, produced substantial and often quite valuable products, usually Association booklets. In recent years, this type of programming has given way to largely staff-directed projects related to curriculum programs. A clear gain has been timely, efficient contributions to Association policy or products. A significant loss, even if apparent mostly to long-time Association members, has been the absolute and symbolic reduction in member participation through Association working groups.

Several recent staff-directed programs have contributed in major ways. A curriculum policy analysis effort, one of these recent programs, has produced several major statements, the first focused on consequences of increased graduation requirements in mathematics and science. This effort has fostered in affiliate groups and in school systems attention to contributions and methodology of curriculum policy analysis. The ASCD high school project, another example of recent programming, focused on cooperative revision of general education programs in high schools during an era when most national attention was prominently focused on proposals for revision. Both a futures project, again involving selected high schools across the nation, and an elementary school project were launched following the three years of the high school project. All of these projects involved curriculum leaders, principals, and teachers from individual schools. Their work has been featured in publications and at annual conferences. Another example of recent programming is the International Conference on Core Curriculum (General Education) in Western Societies at Enschede, the Netherlands, in 1985. This conference served to mark ASCD's significant involvement in an increased international outreach.

The annual conference remains a major membership offering of the Association. Valued differently over the years by individuals, its general worth is seldom questioned. Its scheduled sessions probably reflect the quality and intensity of curriculum development and instructional improvement efforts in the nation's schools. The commentary offered and discussions fostered, many at formal and nonscheduled times, continue to indicate the Association's concern for an intellectual underpinning of practice and for sensitive awareness of contemporary social concerns.

As noted before, ASCD publications and programs do not constitute curriculum development in themselves. They properly may be seen as offerings for the continuing professional education of curriculum and instruction leaders as well as for the production of knowledge about curriculum development and supervison. The breadth of ASCD offerings, the vision of choice of topics and formats, and the quality of descriptions and analyses seem reasonable criteria for the assessment of their potential for affecting school practice and theory. ASCD's recent past manifests conspicuous attention to many members' needs and to opportunities for organizational influence.

A Personal Comment

This review of curriculum-related activities of the past 20 years confirms my belief in the efficacy of ASCD's purposes and programs. The Association is very different now, in many ways, from the one I joined in 1951 when I was a newly appointed elementary school principal. It differs from the ASCD that I served as member of the headquarters staff a decade later, as a member of governance bodies in the 1960s and '70s, and as president only a few years ago. Change, to be sure, is apparent, and stability also is recognized. Evidence of both abounds. ASCD continues to provide access to the intellectual and social ferment surrounding curriculum development issues, proposals and practice, opportunities for shared and increased understanding of issues and personal roles, and a forum for advocacy and disputation. And it does this for increasingly more people each year. In ASCD, people and ideas have always been important. They still are, but in different formats and in ranging degrees.

11

ASCD and the Years Ahead

GORDON CAWELTI
Executive Director

ASCD's growth from 12,000 to 70,000 members over the past dozen years reflects a similarly growing recognition that leaders in education must be more knowledgeable about curriculum and instructional matters than they have been in the past. Pressure has come from parents and politicians alike for schools to serve all youth better, particularly those who leave school ill-prepared for either higher education or work. ASCD has increasingly been recognized as the one organization whose primary interests are of an instructional nature. To meet the professional needs of its increasingly diverse membership, ASCD has undertaken new efforts or expanded existing projects.

The National Curriculum Study Institutes, for instance, are now offered year-round throughout the country to facilitate attendance by more members. Institutes offer a wide range of topics dealing with issues analysis, training, and research, and are attended by 3,000 to 4,000 persons per year.

In what started as a modest effort to capitalize on the new and versatile videotape technology, ASCD's videos are now a vital resource for educators. Estimating an average audience of 100 persons for each of the 9,549 videos that were sold and rented last year, we can assume that nearly a million educators viewed ASCD videotapes in fiscal year 1985.

As state legislatures have become more and more active in educational policy matters in a "reform" era, we have initiated a modest policy analysis effort in which scholars and practitioners examine the consequences of enacted changes in laws and regulations and anticipate the consequences of ideas or policy changes under consideration.

For many members, *Educational Leadership* and other publications remain the flagship of ASCD. In addition, the annual conference, attended by approximately 10 percent of the membership, is the most comprehensive instructional conference of its kind in the country, presenting each year a broad array of topics and expert speakers.

What Shall We Be?

While these new and traditional programs are those most visible to members, they tend not to describe the "soul" of the organization, and the rich mix of professionals that constitute ASCD are by no means near consensus on what the "driving force" or "mission" ought to be. Their interests range from preschool to adult learning modalities, from the scholarly and speculative to the practical and proven. Indeed, perhaps the closest to a mission statement I've heard over the years was from a prominent superintendent who told me that while he was no longer active in ASCD, he continued to urge his staff to be, since he always thought of ASCD as "the conscience of education."

With regard to the theoretical/practical continuum of member viewpoints, we no doubt do more that would be regarded as practical in our institutions, publications, and policy work since the vast majority of our members are practitioners. On the other hand, we have a number of members who are quite good at getting others to *think* about practice, to *question* tradition, and to *search* for values and meaning in what they do. Our contribution in curriculum and instructional theory is notoriously limited, principally because the tangible results of work on theory that are submitted to us are limited in quantity and shallow in substance. We hope our newly established scholarly *Journal of Curriculum and Supervision* will provide an avenue for developing a stronger theory base for these fields.

The ASCD commitment to an open membership is the marketing expert's dream but a significant problem for our governance and staff. While we attract several thousand new members each year, we also lose several thousand persons who presumably look elsewhere for more attention to their particular levels of interest or specialization. It is virtually impossible to avoid such attrition when diversity is valued, as it must be, in the curriculum field.

The Process of Looking Ahead

For several years ASCD operated under a five-year plan that was updated periodically. In 1983, the Executive Council adopted a

1983-1988 plan following involvement of the Board of Directors and a sampling of members' viewpoints. In June 1985, the plan was revised to provide direction for the 1985-1990 period. In contrast to previous plans, the current plan was developed in a more strategic manner that involved analyses of various social trends, closer examination of member composition and interests, and development of six areas of focus, details and provisions of which shall be developed each year.

Before discussing directions that are to be taken during the last half of the decade, it may be instructive if not provocative to consider ideas we decided to reject. While I regard these proposals as legitimate to the purposes of ASCD, several factors weighed heavily against their adoption:

1. There was no great press in their support from members or governance.

2. They involved more risk-taking or nontraditional activities.

3. Ensuring success would be complex to manage.

Association management has become a highly competitive field, resources are always scarce, and the payoff to members in some of these areas might not be apparent. What exactly are these areas that we *might* have pursued?

• *Evaluate curriculum materials, computer or video software, or textbooks in general.* I hold at the moment of this writing a proposal for ASCD to "acquire" a prominent journal that does this reasonably well, but making a decision to proceed is a risky and complex matter.

• *Work much more aggressively than we currently do to influence national, state, and local policy issues.* It is clear to me that the National School Boards Association has determined to play the role of advocacy of lay control. To this end, NSBA spends millions on Capitol Hill and in the courts to ensure a visible presence as educational issues of any kind are deliberated. Their statements on any and all matters ensure that their "presence" is felt.

·• *Extend ASCD's professional influence on an international basis.* For example, our excellent publications program has limited influence in Third World and other non-English-speaking countries, but it could be more influential if we aggressively sought to expand our activities in other parts of the world and provide translated versions of our materials. We *did* determine that modest expansion like that of our affiliate units in Germany, England, and Canada should continue in Europe and the Far East. To this end, ASCD helped to support an international seminar on the core curriculum in Holland in the fall of 1985.

I did not personally press for these ideas to be more strongly considered primarily because we were undergoing a major reorganization of ASCD and engaged in the construction of a new headquarters facility while continuing rapid expansion of membership. Organizations can only sustain so much change, and major new initiatives require careful planning and extensive staff time along with risk capital. When these activities or elements have stabilized, these proposals should be seriously considered for inclusion in an updated long-range plan.

What's Ahead for 1985-1990?

The end result of the process of updating the long-range plan included (1) developing a mission statement, (2) articulating a set of basic planning principles to continually guide our planning efforts, and (3) selecting six areas of new or continued attention in the next few years.

• *Mission Statement.* Virtually any strategic planning process will advocate that the organization clarify in a succinct statement that which does or should characterize its "driving force" or primary role. No institution can be all things to all people and do them well; according to current corporate studies, the most successful businesses are those having reasonable consensus on what they want to be "known for" or "good at." After much discussion, the Executive Council approved the mission statement contained in *Developing Leadership for Quality in Education for All Students.* To make this meaningful, such a statement must be regularly revisited, interpreted, and re-evaluated as a range of current or contemplated activities are considered.

• *Principles Guiding Long-Range Planning.* These principles grew out of an effort to recognize many suggestions and our own realization that it is important to conceive of how we would like the organization to look in the future. At a recent staff retreat, we spent considerable time on just two principles, which resulted in some very productive ideas. This same activity must be undertaken by the Executive Council from time to time if these principles are to become actual descriptors of ASCD in the future. The guiding principles include:

1. *Focus.* Assure a more sustained focus of ASCD resources on a limited number of issues.

2. *Visibility.* Strengthen the visibility and influence of ASCD.

3. *Research.* Increase research emphasis through analysis, synthesis, and dissemination; use research in developmental work in

curriculum, teaching, and learning; identify and foster needed research.

4. *Innovation*. Shorten response time on emerging issues or problems; engage in more innovative or "cutting edge" activities.

5. *Training*. Improve Human Resource Development activities.

6. *Participation*. Increase the number of members actively participating in ASCD activities.

We believe these to be key principles that we hope will characterize our organization in 1990. They need frequent attention and cultivation to bring about significant results.

Six Areas of Focus for 1985-1990

Diverse activities of the Association will continue during this period. Our selection of particular areas of focus does not mean that we will abandon our long-established conventional publications, conference, or policy work.

To identify areas of focus, we spent considerable time on "environmental scanning" and, quite simply, asking members what they saw as emerging issues needing leadership from ASCD. In other words, each area of focus can be traced to one or more social, learning, or political trend that we believe suggests the kinds of activities we envision. Staff liaison persons and officers have been or will be assigned to become "advocates" or planners who will ensure that attention and follow-through are provided.

The areas selected for focus are:

1. *Education and Care of Young Children*. As a result of changing family structures that place more young children in institutional care, and recognition of the efficacy of early intervention in appropriate ways, this focus will put ASCD more fully into a leadership role in the area of early childhood education in identifying learning and policy issues.

2. *Thinking Skills*. Recognizing that we are already an Information Society and that instruction tends toward the lowest order of educational outcomes, this area of focus will enable continuation of several significant contributions ASCD is making in helping to teach for higher-order educational outcomes.

3. *Redefining the Teaching Profession*. Primarily as a result of political pressure from outside the profession, some 15 states have enacted "career ladder" plans for differentiated roles of teachers. This clearly will affect the role of supervisors and compel a whole new cadre of teachers to possess a new set of instructional leadership skills as they advance along the "steps" of these ladder plans.

4. *Emerging Knowledge of Effective Leadership and Supervisory Behavior.* According to studies from the corporate world and on effective leader behavior in schools, educators are demanding more recognition for good work, more growth opportunities, and more authentic involvement in those decisions that affect their professional role. While *knowledge* of these needs is not so new, the demand to accommodate them in the work place is coming from people who are better educated and less subservient than in the past.

5. *Proficiency in Mathematics and Communication as Tools for Learning in a Balanced Curriculum.* Continued public concern over ill-prepared graduates has resulted in a sustained "back-to-basics" movement that is compelling many members to seek more effective ways of ensuring student proficiency if our noble social experiment in educating everyone is to succeed. What is the content of a balanced curriculum that is appropriate for the 21st century?

6. *Technology and the Content and Process of Education.* What role should ASCD play in what many believe to be a revolution in how we retrieve, process, and use information? Because there is a tremendous variety of activity by many organizations in this field, strategic planning for what ASCD will do is essential.

Conclusion

The updated plan also establishes membership targets for 1990 (85,000) and points toward expansion in conference and NCSI attendance. We anticipate increased participation in the important work of the affiliates, which must collaborate more closely with national activities if the principle of increased ASCD visibility and influence is to be attained.

In the final analysis, courageous leadership will be required from governance groups and the staff to fundamentally shift the direction of a major organization like ASCD as it attempts to respond to its members' interests and accurately sense major national trends, the effects of which must be shaped in constructive fashion. The legacy of ASCD will rest on our insightfulness, verve, and willingness to take appropriate risks.

About the Authors

William M. Alexander (ASCD President, 1959-60) is a Professor Emeritus in the Department of Educational Leadership, University of Florida, where he has served in various other positions since 1963. He now teaches intermittently there and at Appalachian State University, where he is a Visiting Professor of Education. Alexander has had extensive public school experience as teacher, curriculum director, administrator, and consultant and has received awards from the American Educational Research Association, the National Association of Secondary School Principals, and the National Middle School Association. His extensive publications include *The Emergent Middle School* (co-authored with Williams and others, 1968 and 1969), *Curriculum Planning* (1954, 1966, and 1974 with Saylor, and 1981 with Saylor and Lewis), and *The Exemplary Middle School* (1981 with George), all published by Holt, Rinehart, and Winston, Inc.

Prudence Bostwick (ASCD President, 1954-55) graduated from Wellesley College and began her career in the Denver, Colorado, Public Schools as a classroom teacher and, later, a supervisor in curriculum development. As a member of the faculty of the California State University at Northridge, Bostwick served as professor of education, specializing in the teaching of English. She became involved in the study of group dynamics and in human relations education as an avocation. While working on her master's degree at the University of Denver, she co-authored with Levette Davidson an anthology titled *The Literature of the Rocky Mountain West 1803-1903*, which has recently been reprinted by the Kennikat Press. She received her Ph.D. from the University of Ohio.

Gordon Cawelti has been Executive Director of the Association for Supervision and Curriculum Development since 1973. Earlier he served as a science teacher and principal in Iowa and as superintendent of the Tulsa, Oklahoma, Public Schools. He has published some 75 articles on curriculum and leadership, as well as the 1984 book, *Redefining General Education in the American High School*.

His major research was a study of innovations in 6,700 high schools, including attention to both adoption and abandonment.

Arthur W. Combs (ASCD President, 1966-67) is a partner in Community Counseling Associates, an educational and psychological consulting firm in Greeley, Colorado. He has been Professor of Education and Psychology at Syracuse University, the University of Florida, and Distinguished Professor at the University of Northern Colorado. He has a long history of contributions to psychology and education—as teacher, administrator, writer, and consultant to schools and colleges in every state. Combs is the author of 22 books and over 150 articles. Best known of his books are *Perceiving, Behaving, Becoming* (1962 ASCD yearbook), *Individual Behavior, Helping Relationships, The Professional Education of Teachers, Myths in Education,* and *A Personal Approach to Teaching.*

O. L. Davis, Jr. (ASCD President, 1982-83), is Professor of Curriculum and Instruction, the University of Texas at Austin. Previously, he was a member of the faculties of Kent State University and the University of North Carolina at Chapel Hill. He has been an elementary and secondary school teacher, a supervising teacher, elementary school principal, and consultant. He has served as an officer of the American Educational Research Association, the Society for the Study of Curriculum History, Kappa Delta Pi, as well as ASCD. He was the first recipient of the NCSS Citation for Exemplary Research in Social Studies Education. Davis has authored and co-authored some 150 publications, including *Exploring the Social Sciences* (1970), *Perspectives on Curriculum Development, 1776-1976* (1976), *The Social Studies* (1981), and *Learning from Student Teaching: A Handbook* (1985). He has also served in an editorial capacity for the *Encyclopedia of Educational Research,* the *American Education Research Journal, The Education Forum,* and the *Journal of Curriculum and Supervision.* He has, as well, led education study seminars in Japan, China, the Soviet Union, Ecuador, and England.

Gerald R. Firth (ASCD President, 1986-87) is Professor and Chairman of the Department of Curriculum and Supervision at the University of Georgia. He has served in leadership positions at the University of Alabama, University of Minnesota, and State University of New York at Buffalo. He has also been a teacher, principal, superintendent, laboratory high school director, and principal investigator for a Ford Foundation project on rural schools, and has served as a consultant both here and overseas. He is the author of numerous articles published in major professional journals and chapters in ASCD yearbooks as well as co-author of two textbooks, *The Curriculum Continuum in Perspective* (1973, published by F. E. Peacock, Inc.) and *Instructional Supervision: A Behavior System* (1975, 1983, published by Allyn and Bacon, Inc.).

Jack Frymier (ASCD President, 1972-73) is a Senior Fellow at Phi Delta Kappa, International, in Bloomington, Indiana. Previously he was a member of the faculty of Curriculum and Foundations at the Ohio State University. He has been a high school social studies teacher and a director of instruction in the Florida public schools. Frymier is the author of many articles in professional journals and author or co-author of several books, including *One Hundred Good Schools* and *Annehurst Curriculum Classification System*.

Alice Miel (ASCD President, 1953-54) is a Professor Emeritus, Teachers College, Columbia University, now living in Gainesville, Florida. After teaching at all levels of the Michigan public schools and serving as a K-12 curriculum coordinator, she earned the doctorate of education at Teachers College and then joined the faculty. She has had numerous overseas consultancies in Puerto Rico, Japan, Uganda, Tanzania, and Afghanistan. From 1973-77, Miel was Executive Secretary of the World Council for Curriculum and Instruction. She has authored and co-authored a number of books, including *Changing the Curriculum—A Social Process* (1946), *Cooperative Procedures in Learning* (1952), *Creativity in Teaching* (1962), and *Supervision for Improved Instruction* (1972).

Phil C. Robinson (ASCD President, 1984-85) is Principal of Clarence B. Sabbath School in River Rouge, Michigan. A former Adjunct Professor at Eastern Michigan University, Robinson has also taught in Detroit and River Rouge and served as supervising principal for student teachers from Eastern Michigan University, Wayne State, and the University of Michigan, Dearborn. He is the author of numerous articles published in state and national journals and has contributed to several books. In 1984, Robinson received the Marcus E. Foster Distinguished Educator Award from the National Alliance of Black School Educators and in 1985 was named Educator of the Year by the Wayne State University chapter of Phi Delta Kappa and Outstanding Practicing Principal by the Michigan Elementary and Middle School Principals Association. It was during his term as ASCD President that Robinson initiated the successful Year of the Teacher project.

J. Galen Saylor (ASCD President, 1965-66) is Professor Emeritus of Education, University of Nebraska-Lincoln. He served on the faculty of the University from 1940 to 1971 and was Chairman of the Department of Secondary Education for 19 years. Previously, he was Director of Research, Nebraska State Education Association, and a public school teacher, principal, and superintendent. He served in the U. S. Navy from 1943 to 1946. A Fulbright Professor at the University of Jyvaskyla, Finland, in 1962-63, Saylor has authored and co-authored 13 books and scores of booklets, articles, yearbook chapters, and encyclopedia articles. He and his wife have traveled in 35 foreign countries.

William Van Til (ASCD President, 1961-62), Coffman Distinguished Professor Emeritus of Education, Indiana State University, has taught and/or administered at the Ohio State University School; the Bureau for Intercultural Education, University of Illinois; George Peabody College; and New York University. He has served as President of the John Dewey Society, the National Society of College Teachers of Education, and ASCD. The author of well over 250 publications (he's stopped counting), Van Til lists his favorites as *The Danube Flows Through Fascism: 900 Miles in a Foldboat* (1938) and *My Way of Looking At It: An Autobiography* (1983), although he is better known for his college textbooks, yearbooks, and columns. Currently he writes and conducts workshops based on his *Writing for Professional Publication* (1986 edition) when not wintering in Puerto Rico.